FORGIVENESS

FORGIVENESS

21 Days to Forgive Everyone for Everything

IYANLA Vanzant

SMILEYBOOKS

Distributed by Hay House, Inc.
Carlsbad, California • New York City
London • Sydney • Johannesburg
Vancouver • New Delhi

DEDICATION

This book is dedicated to
my mother Sahara Elizabeth,
my grandmothers Rissie Holloway and Laura Gill Jefferson,
my stepmother Lynnette May Brown-Harris,
my aunt Nancy McCullum,
my sister Leola Ijalu McCullum-Opeodu,
and all the women who have mothered me
throughout my life.

I forgive my mind for thinking and myself for believing
that who you were and what you gave me was not enough,
was not right, and was not exactly what I needed.

I forgive myself for judging the women who mothered me.

Everything that happens to me is part of the plan for my awakening, including those challenging events that force me to shift out of my inertia and self-limiting behavior patterns. From the depth of my soul, I call out for growth. I pray to be released from my burdens and to discover and express my gifts. From deep within my pain, I call for peace. From deep within my co-dependency, I call for the courage and the freedom to be myself, to forgive myself, and to forgive all others.

—PAUL FERRINI, *EVERYDAY WISDOM*

Contents

WELCOME, BELOVED!

We are about to embark on an exciting and life-changing journey. For some of us, this trek will be as challenging as climbing up a steep mountain while carrying a hundred pounds on our backs. For others, it will be like having a tooth extracted without Novocain. For many of us—those of us who are ready to change, heal, and grow—we will be energized and sometimes shocked with joy over how much we learn about ourselves and how good we begin to feel in the process. We are about to dive headfirst, soul deep into the practice of forgiveness.

What I have learned during my 30-year sojourn through the science of personal and spiritual growth and healing is that forgiveness will cure whatever ails you. The other thing I am totally convinced of is that while forgiveness ain't easy, it's the most important inner work you can do within your mind and heart.

Most of us were never taught that any experience that comes into your life comes by energetic invitation. For this reason, it is imperative that you learn how to keep your energy clear. The practice of forgiveness is your ticket to clarity, vitality, and freedom.

Over the years, I have received hundreds of thousands of letters written by people from all walks of life. Many reveal excruciating stories of sorrow and suffering. At one time, I would write long responses, offering condolences and possible explanations for the tragedies people had endured. Then my daughter passed away, and I was inconsolable. I ended a 40-year relationship, and I was enraged. I was forced to move out of my dream home, and I was ashamed and degraded.

If you know anything about my life story, you know that I have been to some very dark places. Through every experience of my "life breakdown," the only thing that made me feel as if I was still in possession of my right mind, with the capacity to make it through the darkness, was forgiveness. Now, I am sharing what I learned through those experiences with you.

Even when I didn't know whom to forgive or why I should forgive, I said the words. I wrote them in my journal. I cried and screamed, pouted and sometimes I even stomped my feet in resistance, but in the end I learned to forgive everyone for everything, including myself. In the process, I discovered something extraordinary. I discovered peace.

> THIS BOOK IS MY LOVING CHALLENGE FOR YOU TO COME OUT OF THE DARKNESS AND INTO THE LIGHT.

This book is my loving challenge for you to come out of the darkness and into the light. This "21 Days to Forgive Everyone for Everything" practice is my formal invitation for you to join me in an intensive personal transformation process. It's a multidimensional ritual that will clear the decks of your mind and heart to create the space necessary for you to live with more love for yourself and others. This practice will help you achieve a deeper sense of peace and well-being and gain increased clarity about the lessons and blessings available to you. It is my way of walking with you through the twists and turns of your life so that you can discover the hidden path to whatever your heart desires.

I can promise you that if you take this journey with me, you will learn a great deal about yourself, and that is always a good thing. I can also promise that if you hang in there with me, you will begin to see yourself, your life, your every experience, and every person in your life from a new point of view.

Even though I will be with you every step of the way on this journey, I have also invited some friends to join us. When you walk with friends it can make a challenging or difficult journey seem a lot shorter and a great deal easier. At the beginning of selected day's practice, you will meet a "forgiveness friend," a contributor, who will share their story of transformation. From losing a mother in a murder to the reconciliation of siblings, each story reveals that as Reinhold Niebuhr says, "Forgiveness is the final form of love." Forgiveness can do that. It can sharpen and broaden your vision. Then, the vision will pull you forward into a totally new way of being, seeing, and living. I promise you, we can do this—if we do it together.

We can do this if you make the commitment now. We can do this if you are ready to stop feeling bad; stop being wounded; stop wondering why this or that; stop holding grudges; and stop giving yourself reasons and excuses to be, do, and have less than you desire. We can do this if you are ready to experience a miracle in your life. Now remember, this is not easy, but it is doable. So get yourself a beautiful Forgiveness Journal and a special pen, and *let's begin!*

Much love 2 u!
Iyanla

P.S.: This book is accompanied by a free audio download. You'll find the download link and track list on pages 322 and 323. Don't miss it.

— PART I —

THE PRACTICE

WHY FORGIVE?

You might be asking yourself, "Why would I want to practice forgiveness?" The answer is simple. Practice develops skill. Skill leads to mastery. When you master the practice of forgiveness, it becomes as natural as breathing. And when you know how to forgive, you eliminate excess mental and emotional weight that keeps you stuck in repetitive situations, circumstances, and experiences that are not healthy or productive.

The only true way to create a more loving, productive, and fulfilling life is by forgiving the past. Releasing the past restores us to the full energy of the present moment.

Everything we do and experience in life is born from the energy we carry. People and experiences show up in response to the conscious and unconscious energetic invitations we issue. Many of us believe that what happens to us gives rise to the feelings we experience. The truth is, it's the other way around.

Forgiveness addresses how we think and feel about others and ourselves, and how those thoughts manifest within our lives as energy. Every feeling has its origin in a thought, because each thought that we have creates energy. If you can remove the thought, the underlying feeling will bubble to the surface. That's why we are forgiving our thoughts throughout this process.

As Michael Grant, author of *The Twelve Laws of Life,* reminds us, "Your mind controls your mood. In fact, it is safe to say that you always have some thought (mind) before you feel something emotionally (mood). The thought might be so fast and seemingly 'automatic' that you don't even see it or think you are thinking it but you are. The truth is that what you think determines what you feel—it's a basic law of life."

If you can tap into and identify the feeling, you will discover that there's a thought linked to it. Once you remove the feeling, the thought will also dissipate. Whether you explore the source thought or the feeling doesn't matter. What matters is, if a situation, circumstance, or relationship doesn't feel good, that's a sign that there's someone or something you have to forgive.

It's all about energy. The true and pure energy of life, good, and God is positive energy. In this practice we deal with the thought because the mind is a powerful, creative energy. Everything we think, do, and feel begins in the mind. For this reason, we have to address the thoughts, beliefs, judgments, learnings, and perceptions that we hold in our minds. When we can identify the stuck feelings underneath our constant thoughts and neutralize them, we will be good. Forgiveness helps to transform and eliminate the energy blockages that we hold in our minds about who we are and who others are, and the subsequent issues or upsets that grow from the thoughts, beliefs, and judgments we hold. Creating a loving, healthy, and fulfilling life plus loving, healthy, and fulfilling relationships begins in the mind.

Many of us live in our heads because feelings can be frightening. It's easier to stay in our heads thinking, believing, and judging, since doing so seems safer than navigating through uncomfortable feelings. I refer to folks who live like this as "neck-down-dead!" because there's no life below the neck. They think about everything and often come across as cold, detached, and unfeeling, and in many cases, they are just that.

The energy of a feeling doesn't die or go away because we ignore or resist it. In fact, it is the energy of the unacknowledged feeling beneath the distorted thoughts that keeps us stuck. Our feelings send harmonious or disharmonious energy signals throughout our bodies. Yet if we drop our hands to our sides, sit in the feeling for a moment, and just breathe instead of numbing out, the feeling will pass. Too often, we choose to avoid feelings because they frighten us. But once we learn how to harness the energy behind our thoughts, our emotions will no longer be in control of how we feel and what we do. Forgiveness is a practice that helps us to realign our thoughts and feelings under new conscious management.

Think of it this way: the mind is like a little puppy. A puppy will run around all over the place until we train him to do otherwise. If we don't train the puppy, he'll grow into a full-grown dog that will pee on the carpet, chew on our shoes, and hump our guests. When we train our own "puppy mind" to sit, stay, and roll over on command, our thoughts become clearer and our negative feelings become easier to identify, navigate, and release.

Of course, training the mind can be difficult. That's where meditation and forgiveness come into play. These two practices—meditation and forgiveness—still the "puppy mind" so that the energy blocked in our bodies can bubble up to the surface and be released. Until we learn how to meditate, we cannot clear our "puppy mind" thoughts. And unless we practice forgiveness, we have no way of releasing the hidden feelings attached to those thoughts.

Quite often we are stuck in the memories of what we have done or not done; what others have done to us or not done for us. How we think and feel about others and ourselves can keep us stuck in a swamp of toxic emotions. More often than not, we're self-righteous about what we think and feel. We become quick to judge and slow to forgive. We believe what we believe, and we stubbornly stick to it. Unfortunately, our toxic thoughts and feelings do not nurture or nourish us, nor do they make or keep us peaceful and loving.

> FORGIVENESS ADDRESSES HOW WE THINK AND FEEL ABOUT OTHERS AND OURSELVES AND HOW THOSE THOUGHTS MANIFEST WITHIN OUR LIVES AS ENERGY.

I offer you this simple formula for recognizing discordant thoughts and feelings. *First you think, then you feel, and finally you hold the energy in your body.* For example, if you think that you have been or are being abandoned, you may feel the need to hold on to things and people. As a result, you may act clingy or needy, which will chase people away from you, and that will in turn prompt even greater feelings of abandonment within you.

Neck-down-dead people, those who refuse to feel their true feelings, will do just the opposite. Rather than deal with their repressed thoughts and feelings of abandonment, they refuse to become attached in the first place. They come across as cold and hard-hearted, which also chases others away.

> FORGIVENESS BUILDS MENTAL, EMOTIONAL, AND SPIRITUAL MUSCLES.

They escalate their disowned feelings and re-create the same painful experiences over and over again. Unfortunately, the "neck-down-dead" like to lay their issues at the feet of other people and project their unprocessed thoughts /feelings onto everybody else.

Practicing forgiveness will heal the original experience of abandonment that has resulted in the subsequent detachment from feelings. Our work in this forgiveness practice will be to get to the underbelly of the experience in order to release the thoughts and feelings that perpetuate the merry-go-round ride. Forgiveness is a process that stops the ride and eliminates the wounds of the past from the mind and the heart. Forgiveness supports our growth into a new way of thinking, being, and living. Forgiveness builds mental, emotional, and spiritual muscles. In today's world, *muscle*—i.e., strength and endurance—is something we can all use a lot more of each and every day.

Throughout this forgiveness practice, you will be asked to identify thoughts and beliefs. A belief is a thought—fueled by a feeling—that you think over and over until it becomes habitual. Once a thought becomes habitual, you no longer even recognize that you are thinking it. For this reason, it is absolutely essential to identify and release the long-held, worn-out beliefs that often hold toxic thoughts in place. For the neck-down-dead people, such revelations may be a bit challenging. No worries, though! I've got you covered.

EMOTIONAL TRIGGERS

Sometimes identifying the thoughts, feelings, beliefs, and judgments you may need to forgive is not easy. The intuitive tool that follows is designed to assist you in tapping into and receiving feedback from the subconscious mind about the unforgiving and often hidden aspects of your consciousness. These are the things that may block, delay, hinder, obstruct, or deny personal growth and healing. They are also the things that lower your personal energy vibration. Identifying and forgiving these energetic blockages is essential for personal evolution.

This list is in no way exhaustive; however, it covers most of the common and habitual feelings that the average person experiences without even thinking about it. When you come to the belief-clearing portion of your forgiveness practice, this list may prove to be invaluable, as it will help you identify the feeling that is hidden beneath the thought.

Scan the Emotional Trigger List quickly across one line at a time. If a word catches your attention, write it down. While many of the entries may not seem to apply to you, be sure to scan the list each day before you tackle the forgiveness topic of the day and begin writing your 12 Forgiveness Statements.

For example, be sure to scan the Emotional Trigger List before engaging the Forgiveness Practice for forgiving your mother, your father, and, yes, even God. Remember to be radically honest with yourself and about how you feel. Do not judge ("I shouldn't think/feel this way") or be concerned about how many triggers actually apply to your thoughts and feelings about yourself or other people.

Review the following Emotional Trigger words to help you identify all of the blocks that may be present in your heart and/or mind. Just know that judgments and energy blockages exist when:

> I believe I am . . .
> I believe he/she/they are . . .
> I think/I feel/I anticipate/I avoid
> the following Emotional Triggers

Abandoned	Absentminded	Abuse	Accidents
Accusing	Addicted	Afraid	Aggravated
Aggressive	Agitated	Agony	Alone
Ambition	Analyzing	Anger	Anguish
Anxiety	Apprehensive	Arguing	Arrogance
Ashamed	Ashamed (of self/life)	Attachment	Attack (of self/life)

Avoidance	Bad	Being judgmental	Being opinionated
Being reactive	Being scattered	Being too emotional	Being ungrounded
Betrayed	Bitterness	Blaming	Blind devotion
Bored	Boredom	Bossiness	Burdened
Busyness	Carelessness	Cheated (out of something)	Codependency
Complaining	Compromise	Compulsion	Concerned
Conflict	Conflicted	Confused	Confusion
Control	Control (Loss of)	Controlling	Cowardice
Crazy	Critical	Criticism	Criticized
Cruelty	Cynical	Deceitfulness	Deception
Deceptive	Defeated	Defensive	Defensiveness
Defiance	Dejected	Denial	Denied
Dependency	Depression	Desperate	Despondent
Destructive	Devastated	Deviousness	Discontent
Discounted	Discounting	Discouraged	Disgraced
Dishonesty	Dismay	Disorder	Disoriented
Dominance	Doubt	Doubt (in self)	Drained
Drama	Dread	Dreaming	Egotistical
Embarrassed	Emotions	Emptiness (in life)	Empty (within self)
Enraged	Entitled (to more)	Envy	Escape
Exaggeration	Excessive focus on others	Excuses	Exploited

Extremist	Failure	Fake	False
Fantasizing	Fatigued physical/mental	Faulty beliefs	Fearful
Fears	Feeling needy	Fixed ideas	Focusing on the past
Foolishness	Forgetful	Fragmented	Frightened
Grief	Guilt	Gullible	Heartache
Heartbroken	Heartsick	Heaviness (of burdens)	Heavy in mind or body
Helpless	Hesitant	Hopeless	Horrified
Hostile	Humiliated	Hurried	Hurt
Impulsiveness	Inaccuracy	Inadequate	Incomplete
Indebted	Indecision	Indifference	Indifferent
Indignant	Inertia	Inflexible	Injury
Insecurity	Insensitivity	Intellectualization	Intolerance
Invalidated	Irresponsible	Irritated	Isolation
Jealousy	Judged	Judgmental	Justifying limitations
Lack of commitment	Lack of confidence	Lack of creativity	Lack of discipline
Lack of energy	Lack of purpose	Lack of trust	Laziness
Lazy	Living in the past	Loneliness	Lonely
Lost	Low energy	Lying	Mad
Malnutrition	Manipulated	Manipulation	Martyrdom

Materialism	Mediocrity	Melancholy	Minimizing
Miserable	Misunderstood	Moodiness	Mortified
Narrowness	Needing to please others	Negativity	No fun
Nonsupportive habits	Numbed out	Numbness	Obligated
Obsessions	Offended	Opportunism	Outraged
Overeating	Overexercise	Overextended	Overlooked
Overspending	Overweight	Overwhelm	Overwhelmed
Overwork	Pain	Perfectionism	Persecuted
Phobias	Poor health	Poor self-esteem	Possessiveness
Poverty mentality	Prejudice	Pressured	Pride
Procrastination	Punished	Put down	Put upon
Rage	Rationalization	Rebellion	Rebellious
Regret	Repression	Resented	Resentful
Resentment	Resistance	Responsible	Ridicule
Rudeness	Running away	Sadness	Sarcasm
Scared	Scattered	Scorned	Seeking approval
Self-centeredness	Self-conscious	Self-deception	Self-obsession
Self-righteous	Shattered	Shame about something	Shy
Silly	Sorrow	Stagnant	Struggling
Stuck	Stupid	Suffering	Suspicious
Terrified	Tired	Tortured	Trapped
Traumatized	Troubled	Ugly	Unappreciated

Uncertain	Uncomfortable	Unfocused	Unfulfilled
Unloved	Unmotivated	Unprepared	Unsupported by others
Unsupportive of others	Untrusting (of self/God)	Unworthy	Vengeful
Vulnerable	Wasted	Weak	Weary
Weird	Worn out	Worried	Worthless
Wounded			

JUDGE NOT!

It's funny, just like me, much of America is addicted to TV shows such as *Law & Order, CSI,* or *NCIS.* These crime-and-punishment dramas support our beliefs that everyone and everything must be judged. For every crime there must be a punishment. On any given day, we are all judge and jury in the cases we build or hold on to in our minds.

We judge ourselves and others when we believe someone is guilty until proven innocent. In the realm of consciousness, a judgment is a classification. It is a thought that classifies people and things as right or wrong,

> FORGIVENESS IS THE ONLY CURE FOR LONG-HELD JUDGMENTS.

good or bad, fair or unfair when measured against what we believe. At the core of all judgments there is the belief that things are not as they should be, as we want them to be, or as we need them to be. Our judgments more often than not give rise to a toxic or negative feeling. Forgiveness is the only cure for long-held judgments. Forgiveness of our judgments opens space and energy in our minds and hearts that has been held blocked off by anger, bitterness, and resentment.

What is often challenging for the human mind to accept is that regardless of how hard, challenging, frightening, or difficult an experience may seem, everything is just as it needs to be in order for us to heal, grow, and learn. That's just the way the universe works. Granted, most humans have a very difficult time accepting the way the universe works. This is what it means to be human. This is why we are faced with challenges and difficulties. This is how we ultimately learn to trust the process of life and our capacity to move through the hard times. This is how we grow in faith and learn to trust God.

The moment we determine what is, should not be, we are denying the presence of love. God is love. Love is always present, surrounding us; guiding, growing, and teaching us. Even in the midst of total chaos, pain, and dysfunction, love is calling us to a higher experience and expression.

Forgiveness inevitably leads to acceptance. It is a demonstration of your willingness to move on. Acceptance does not mean you agree with, condone, appreciate, or even like what has happened. Acceptance means that you know, regardless of what happened, that there is something bigger than you at work. It also means *you know that you are okay and that you will continue to be okay.* Even if you don't know it yet, it means you are willing to get to that space: forgiveness restores our faith, rebuilds our trust, and opens our hearts to the presence and power of love.

JUDGMENTS

From the age of 16 until his death on the eve of his 50th birthday, my brother was cross-addicted to drugs and alcohol. When he was sober, Ray was the most gentle, loving, brilliant man I had ever known. He had a wicked sense of humor, and he absolutely loved children. Watching the way he interacted with my children, I was often jealous that I did not have his patience and his capacity to see things in a childlike and innocent manner. When, however, my brother was high, his behavior was belligerent, argumentative, and quite often insulting. I could not for the life of me understand why such a beautiful, handsome, and brilliant man would willingly alter his state of consciousness and knowingly put poison in his body.

> AT THE CORE OF
> ALL JUDGMENTS THERE IS
> THE BELIEF THAT
> THINGS ARE NOT
> AS THEY SHOULD BE,
> AS WE WANT THEM TO BE,
> OR AS WE NEED THEM TO BE.

After many years of late-night telephone calls that ended with one or both of us screaming at the top of our lungs, I put my foot down. I told my brother he was not welcome to call me if he was not sane and sober. In response, he did not call me . . . for five years. During that time I had to think long and hard about how harshly I had judged my big brother. I knew the intricate ins and outs of our childhood. I knew how sensitive my brother was and how deeply he had been hurt, damaged, and wounded by the bad behavior of the adults in our lives. I knew these things about him because I knew the same was true for me.

It took a while and a great deal of self-forgiveness for me to recognize that I, too, was an addict. I didn't drink or do drugs, but I was addicted to external validation, to being right about everything, to having things go my way so that I could feel safe. I had a tendency to say whatever I wanted to whomever, without any regard for the appropriateness or necessity of my speaking. I was addicted to being seen and being heard, and, at the same time, I was addicted to being unacceptable and guilty. About nine months before I heard from my brother, I recognized that I had judged him for the very things I found unacceptable about myself.

Nothing in life causes more pain and suffering than the judgments we hold about and against others and ourselves. I think Byron Katie says it best: "When you argue against reality, you will suffer." Judgments are the thoughts or arguments we hold about or against what is, what was, and what should be. All judgments create suffering and need to be forgiven.

Every interaction and experience in life offers the opportunity to become aware of those things that we do not recognize and/or do not accept about ourselves. This is the foundation of all judgments. It is very easy to point out in others the things we deny, dismiss, avoid, excuse, and resist acknowledging that we actually believe are true about us. When we are willing to be emotionally honest, we will discover that the reactions we have to circumstances, situations, and people give us more information about ourselves than about anyone or anything else. Every upsetting encounter is triggering an emotion that is present on our internal landscape.

> NOTHING IN LIFE CAUSES MORE PAIN AND SUFFERING THAN THE JUDGMENTS WE HOLD ABOUT AND AGAINST OURSELVES.

When someone makes a remark about us, it may trigger hurt or fear or sadness. We may judge the person as mean or insensitive or disrespectful. Upon a closer investigation, it's revealed that the thing being said by someone else is the same thing we may have said to ourselves about ourselves—when no one else was around. However, when a person makes the same remark and we *don't* have that judgment about ourselves, chances are we will not be hurt or offended by it. Regardless of the circumstances, our internal reactions to people and events are a reflection of our own self-judgments and long-held toxic emotions. Rarely do our negative reactions have anything to do with another person's bad behavior.

PRIMARY JUDGMENT ISSUES

More often than not, judgments can be traced back to one of three primary issues:

1. **We do not/cannot tolerate the same behavior or characteristic in ourselves.** When we harbor feelings or inadequacy, inappropriateness, weakness, or the "not-good-enough" syndrome, we resent seeing our behaviors and tendencies demonstrated by another person. Seeing it "out there" embarrasses us, so we condemn what is being demonstrated. A judgment of resentment or embarrassment often reveals that we are not fully expressing ourselves, and we experience resentment or anger when others do so.

2. **We are unaware that we behave a certain way and of the impact that behavior has on others.** So we disown it and project the behavior onto others and dislike it "out there." Whenever we experience dislike, upset, or anger about how someone is being who they are, we must ask ourselves, "How and under what circumstances am I prone to behave the same way?" Only when we become willing to take an honest look within to determine if we share some of the characteristics we dislike in others can we become self-accepting and self-aware.

3. **When we are envious and resentful, we must find something wrong with others who have what we want or do what we desire to do.** We judge them in order to make them wrong about who we are and what we have not created for ourselves. When someone attains a certain level of success or recognition, it may remind us of a lack of confidence or success in our own life experience. When feelings of inadequacy surface in the face of success, chances are we will look for and find something wrong with the person to negate what is right or good about them and their accomplishments. This is also known as the "crabs-in-a-barrel" mentality: pulling someone down to the level we believe we are on.

Since judgments are a strategy used by the ego to avoid uncomfortable feelings, if we are unaware of the feelings hiding on our own internal land-scape, we can and most likely will create all sorts of judgmental stories about the people to distract our attention away from what we are experiencing within. It is only when we forgive our judgments that we can have compassion for others, even when they behave in ways we would not.

Forgiveness allows us to explore and release our long-held beliefs and assumptions about ourselves instead of judging other people. The reward of forgiveness is that it eliminates the trap of unconscious ego gratification that we receive when we judge others and gives rise to a deeper experience of self-understanding. When we truly understand ourselves and cultivate compassion for the less-desirable aspects of who we are, it is highly unlikely that our first reaction will be to judge someone else. What we have more of within and for ourselves, we are free to give more of to others.

Judging people occurs when we watch their actions. The way anyone behaves is a function of their individual understanding of who they are, what is expected, and their historical perspective of life. Often we make judgments about others at a time when we cannot process our own feelings of discomfort. Critical comments about anyone else are always a mirror into our own life and attitudes. With time, practice, and forgiveness we grow a deeper understanding of what we say and do to others that can and will transform how we live within ourselves.

REGARDLESS OF HOW HARD,
CHALLENGING, FRIGHTENING, OR DIFFICULT
AN EXPERIENCE MAY SEEM, EVERYTHING IS
JUST AS IT NEEDS TO BE IN ORDER FOR US
TO HEAL, GROW, AND LEARN.

TAPPING INTO FORGIVENESS

After losing my daughter, I was mentally, emotionally, and spiritually depleted and stuck. I was stuck in sorrow, grief, and rage. The sorrow and grief were understandable. The rage—not so much. I couldn't put my finger on whom I was angry with or what I was angry about; however, the energy of the rage kept me in a constant state of nausea. More than any other emotion, I know the dangerous impact anger has on the nervous system. I knew what to do, how to heal myself. I did not want to do it because I felt I had a right to the anger. After all, I had just buried my beautiful daughter —why shouldn't I be angry? Why? Because anger, rage, sadness, shame, guilt, and every other toxic and unproductive emotion is harmful to your body—that's why. It was the early days of spring. Spring is a time for newness and growth. It was time for me to grow beyond loss and sorrow and sadness and rage. And even though I didn't want to do it, I knew it was time.

One of my morning practices is to sit on my deck, sip my coffee, and read my daily word: inspirational books that help me stay centered and grounded. When I complete my daily reading, I dump my mind by writing in my journal. It was only 60 degrees outside that morning, but the sun was shining, and that always helps me feel better. So that day, I skipped the reading and went right to my journal. I wrote down everything I could think of that made me mad as hell.

Six pages in, I started writing my Forgiveness Statements. I forgave myself for all of the judgments and fears that I had been holding and protecting. Once I had three pages completed, I began to tap myself free of my turbulent thoughts and feelings. The results were so profound that I later became trained and certified as an expert in a healing process known as the Progressive Emotional Freedom Technique (Pro EFT™), or tapping. Pro EFT™, the process created by EFT Master Lindsay Kenny, can be compared to the process of needless acupuncture. This evolution of meridian-based therapy—used to move energetic blockages through and out of the body—is rooted the pioneering work of Gary Craig.

Every thought creates energy or vibrational waves that send messages throughout the body and into the physical environment in which we live. When we have repetitive negative or toxic thoughts, a disruption occurs in our energy pathways that pollutes the body and creates discord in our life experiences. The energy created by our toxic thoughts and emotions is like fuel in a car; it passes through every system and determines the car's performance. Good fuel will keep a car running at maximum capacity. Bad fuel will clog every system until the car breaks down or becomes inoperable. Emotions in the body are like fuel in the car; they will either keep you running smoothly or keep you stuck internally and externally. Being stuck internally can result in all sorts of physical ailments and diseases. Being stuck externally can impact relationships, finances, and the ability to find your path or fulfill your destiny.

We all hold negative energy in the form of thoughts, beliefs, emotions, and memories about someone or something. Not only do these thoughts create stress, they can also trigger a disruption in the body's energy or meridian system that is experienced as a physical or psychological pain. Tapping is a process that can unblock the stuck mental, emotional, or psychological discomfort caused by blocked energy. By tapping on specific meridian points on the body and speaking aloud the thoughts and feelings that we hold, we can stimulate and clear the systems in our body that store blocked energy.

On the following pages is a road map of the energy/meridian tapping points that we will be working with throughout our forgiveness process. It was provided by EFT Master Lindsay Kenny, my teacher, friend, and coach. The Tapping System that we use in our 21-Day Forgiveness Practice is my adaptation of Lindsay's Pro EFT™ system. The Pro EFT™ points are easy to identify and understand, and they can be harnessed to produce miraculous changes in your life.

The Energy Points chart is a helpful reminder of all of the EFT locations on which you will be tapping throughout your forgiveness journey. The Tapping Points Connections chart outlines the deep connections between our energy meridians and our emotions. It underscores why tapping can literally "set us free."

If you're brand new to tapping, please visit www.ProEFT.com where you can access a Basic EFT manual and lots of invaluable resources on the Free Stuff page.

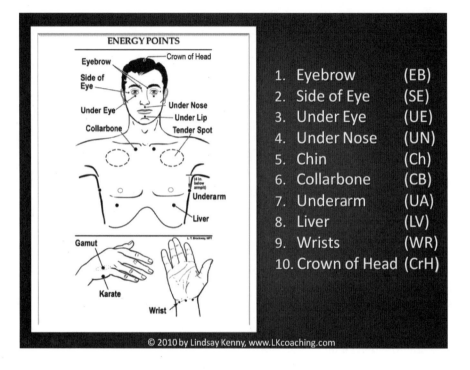

ENERGY POINTS

- Crown of Head
- Eyebrow
- Side of Eye
- Under Eye
- Under Nose
- Under Lip
- Collarbone
- Tender Spot
- Underarm (4 in. below armpit)
- Liver
- Gamut
- Karate
- Wrist

1. Eyebrow   (EB)
2. Side of Eye   (SE)
3. Under Eye   (UE)
4. Under Nose   (UN)
5. Chin   (Ch)
6. Collarbone   (CB)
7. Underarm   (UA)
8. Liver   (LV)
9. Wrists   (WR)
10. Crown of Head (CrH)

Tapping Points Connections:
Meridians and Emotions

Karate Chop Point (KC) *On side of hand* **Small Intestine Meridian**
Releases: sadness, psychological reversal (feeling stuck or frozen), inability to let go, resistance to change, worry, compulsive behavior
Supports: letting go of the past, moving forward, healing from grief, connecting to present circumstances

Eyebrow (EB): *Beginning of eyebrow* **Bladder Meridian**
Releases: trauma, hurt, sadness, restlessness, frustration, impatience, dread
Supports: peace, emotional healing

Side of Eye (SE): *Outer corner* **Gall Bladder Meridian**
Releases: rage, anger, irritation, resentment, fear of change, muddled thinking
Supports: clarity, compassion

Under Eye (UE): *On bone beneath eye* **Stomach Meridian**
Releases: obsessive worry, anxiety, phobias, frustration, nervousness, cravings
Supports: trust, contentment, calmness, feeling safe

Under Nose (UN) *Middle of upper lip* **Governing Meridian through Spinal Column**
Releases: embarrassment, cowardice, powerlessness, shame, guilt, fear of ridicule or failure, deep psychological reversal
Supports: bravery, courage, self-acceptance, self-empowerment

Chin (CH): *Below lower lip* **Central Vessel Channel to the Body**
Releases: shame, confusion, uncertainty, second-guessing decisions, psychological reversal
Supports: honor, clarity, certainty, confidence, self-acceptance

Collarbone (CB): *One inch below actual bones* **Neurolympathic System**
Releases: anxiety, insecurity, indecision, psychological reversal, feeling stuck, general stress
Supports: power and accomplishment, ease in moving forward, reason diplomacy, confidence, clarity, harmony

Underarm (UA): *Middle of armpit* **Spleen Meridian**
Releases: low self-esteem, self-neglect, anxiety, obsession, nervousness, hopelessness
Supports: clarity, confidence, fairness, relaxation, compassion for self and others

Liver (LV): *Directly under breasts* **Liver Meridian**
Releases: rage against self, anger, guilt, unhappiness
Supports: kindness toward self, nurturance, self-acceptance

Wrists (WR): *Center point of wrists* **Heart, Pericardium, and Liver Meridians**
Releases: pain, grief, self-neglect, overwhelm, anger, insomnia, bloating, swelling, emotional/mental stress
Supports: body consciousness, nervous system, relaxation, clear thinking, intuition, transformation, regeneration

Crown of Head (CrH) *Two inches back from direct center* **Governing Meridian**
Releases: compulsive thinking, confusion, disorganization, inner critic
Supports: ability to take a stand, spiritual connection and discernment, insight, intuition, focus, wisdom, clarity

Combining forgiveness and tapping is a powerful way to unclog every system in your life and open the way for new energy and experiences to unfold. The key to successful tapping is being able to identify and speak aloud the emotions attached to the thoughts and memories that are repetitive or stuck. Women hold negative thoughts about women and about men. Men hold negative thoughts about men and about women. Many people hold negative thoughts about blacks, whites, Latinos, or Asians; about their mother, father, supervisor, lover, or child. As you move through the 21-Day Forgiveness Process, it will be important to identify the negative emotions hiding behind your thoughts. You can do this by using the Emotional Triggers List on pages 9–14. By identifying the negative thoughts or toxic feelings associated with the people or experiences you are choosing to forgive, tapping can add even more positive fuel to your life and well-being.

There are powerful, positive rewards that come from forgiveness. Releasing long-held or toxic memories through the forgiveness process—and eliminating the stress that energetic blockages place on your body—can add years to your life. Adding tapping to the forgiveness process opens your energy centers so that you can attract more of what you desire instead of staying stuck in what you already have.

The Forgiveness Tapping Process

- Identify the Issue

- Rate the Intensity Level

- Clearing Resistance/The Reversal Statement

- The Set-Up Statement

- The Tapping Sequence

- Recheck the Intensity Level

Step 1: Identify the Issue

Each day during the 21-Day Forgiveness Process you'll be working through a specific issue. That issue will be the focus of your journal and tapping work for the day. You'll be journaling and tapping away the repetitive thoughts, beliefs, emotions, and memories on the day's topic.

Step 2: Rate the Intensity Level

For this process you'll need to determine the energetic or emotional intensity of day's issue on a scale of 0 to 10. You can do this by simply thinking about the day's issue and asking yourself, "On a scale of 0 to 10, how intense is the energy charge on this issue in my body?" Trust what you hear.

Write the number down.

0 = No energetic charge or distress. I am at peace.

5 = I feel uncomfortable, but I can tolerate it.

10 = This is a real problem, and it's making me feel crazy. I'm in major distress.

Remember that we are going for the gold in our tapping process, aiming for a 0 rating. This means that when you rate your "forgiveness" on each day's topic, the goal is to feel clear, unburdened, peaceful, and complete. Don't worry about getting the right number. Just ask yourself, "On a scale of 0 to 10, what is the intensity level of 'unforgiveness' I have on today's topic?" A number will pop into your mind. Trust what comes forward.

STEPS 3 AND 4: CLEARING RESISTANCE AND THE SET-UP STATEMENT

When something is familiar, even if it's no good for us, the mind has a tendency to hold on to it. Resistance is the mental and emotional act of holding on to what is unproductive or, in many cases, toxic and self-destructive. This means that our conscious intentions are literally reversed, as though we're wired backward. Unfortunately, we are not always aware that we are in resistance. The Reversal Statement and Set-Up Statement are designed to release the subconscious, or even conscious, resistance that keeps us stuck. These statements work to kick long-held habitual or repetitive thoughts and feelings out of the driver's seat and to the curb. Releasing hidden resistances allows our tapping work to progress at a much faster rate.

For the purpose of the 21-Day Forgiveness Process, the Reversal Statements and Set-Up Statements will often be quite similar. At the beginning of each day's tapping sequence, you will repeat the Reversal Statement and the Set-Up Statement each three times while tapping continuously on the Karate Chop point.

Here's the Pro EFT™ Reversal Statement Formula: Even though this _____ (problem, emotion, or lack of forgiveness) causes me to _____ (how it affects your life; keeps you stuck, angry, bitter, stressed, etc.) there's a PART of me that doesn't want to release it (change it, let it go, move on, forgive them, etc.). And I want to love (or accept, respect, like . . .) myself anyway.

It's important to remember that you can't just do the Reversal Setup alone. You then must tap on the rounds until the issue is completely gone . . . not just "better."

Sample Reversal Statement: *Even though there is a part of me that is holding on to [daily topic] and that part of me refuses to let it go, I love myself totally and unconditionally.*

Sample Set-Up Statement: *Even though I have been holding on to unforgiveness and judgments about [the daily topic] and I don't want to let them go, I still deeply and completely love, respect, and accept myself.*

Note that both the Set-Up Statement and later in the process, the Modified Set-Up Statement both contain the word "still." This word signals your subconscious mind that you're in the active release phase of your process.

STEP 5: THE TAPPING SEQUENCE

Throughout the Forgiveness Process you will be tapping on and into a different issue for each of the 21 days. For example, on Day 1 your work will focus on the unforgiveness you have held about yourself. On Day 2, your work will focus on the unforgiveness that you have held about your body.

Daily intentional tapping on each of the 10 meridian points responsible for the positive flow of energy throughout your body, mind, and spirit is a powerful process. To create your own complete Tapping Sequence, known as a Tapping Script, link the 12 Forgiveness Statements written in your daily journal work to your tapping of the 10 meridian points. Your self-created Tapping Script will free stuck energy and restore you to a new level of peace, balance, and equilibrium.

Starting with the Eyebrow and tapping to the Crown of the Head constitutes one round of tapping. As you tap, you'll speak each written Forgiveness Statement out loud as a reminder of your intention. Work on each meridian point until your intensity level has reached 0. Always do a full round—from Eyebrow to Crown of the Head—even if it means you repeat the same statement several times.

STEP 6: RECHECK INTENSITY LEVEL

Once you have completed 3 rounds of tapping on the day's issue, stop and have a few sips of water. Take a deep breath in through your nose. Release the breath slowly and softly through your mouth, making the sound "Ahhhhh" as you do so.

Again, simply ask yourself the question: "On a scale of 0 to 10, how intense is this issue within my body?" Trust what you hear.

Recheck your intensity level on any unforgiveness you are holding about yourself or others.

If the level is at 8 or higher, repeat the entire 3-Round Tapping Sequence outlined in one of the bonus Tapping Scripts (or your self-created script). There are three bonus Tapping Scripts in this 21-Day Forgiveness Practice, including "I Forgive Myself," "I Forgive My Mother," and "I Forgive My Relationship with Money." These bonus scripts offer examples you can follow for creating your own original scripts.

If the level is less than 8, repeat one of the Modified Set-Up Statement 3 times while tapping constantly on the Karate Chop point. This helps to unlock any remain resistance. Then perform the 10-point Tapping Sequence on the 12 Forgiveness Statements from your daily journal work.

Repeat the sequence, pausing after each round to recheck the energetic intensity of your issue. Chart your progress, until you are at a 0 level of intensity.

— PART II —

21 DAYS OF FORGIVENESS

I forgave the man who raped me and the men
who abandoned me.

I forgave the woman who abused me and the
women who betrayed me.

I forgave the people who lied to me and I forgave
those who lied about me.

I forgave the person who stole from me, the person
who disappointed me, and all of the people who
dismissed, diminished, and denied me.

The only person I have not been willing or able to
forgive is myself.

—Iyanla Vanzant

I Forgive Myself

Above all else, I want to see things differently.

I want to see what is true and loving and kind
and real instead of the false thoughts and images I have
projected onto the world and myself.

Forgiveness releases from my mind the false thoughts
making sight, the "seeing," possible.

Forgiveness will undo the image making
of the ego that I have done unto myself.

—Prayer for *A Course in Miracles Workbook*
Lesson 28

– Forgiveness Story by Iyanla Vanzant –

As human beings, it is so easy to identify and judge the bad behavior and wrongdoings of another person. It is far more difficult, and even more important, to see and consider how your *own* prior bad acts have attracted certain people, situations, and experiences into your life. If you are *really* paying attention and *really* ready to heal, the day will come when you recognize that forgiveness is the only way back to the center of your innocence. This is a very hard lesson that I was blessed to learn.

It took four years to reach the point of crisis but only two minutes to drop me to my knees. I suspected for a long time that my granddaughter's father regarded me with total contempt and rage. If the truth were to be told, I more than suspected—I knew. But I simply didn't care. My only concern was my granddaughter, Gemmia's baby girl. I sensed there was a power play at work between my granddaughter's father and me. He was finally in control of something I wanted, and he was doing everything possible to demonstrate his power over me.

> THE DAY WILL COME WHEN YOU RECOGNIZE THAT FORGIVENESS IS THE ONLY WAY BACK . . .

He was withholding my granddaughter. I could see her only when he said so and only if I played by the rules he set. It didn't matter that I called two or three times a week. He returned the calls when he was good and ready, which was usually every two weeks, or if her being with me was convenient for him. I played the game because

I was afraid that if I stepped out of line, I would never get to see her. And I knew that being able to see her was far more important than flexing my muscles.

Things reached the boiling point when he blocked his telephone—she could not call me, and whenever I called, it went straight to voice mail. Six weeks

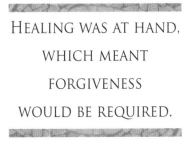

HEALING WAS AT HAND, WHICH MEANT FORGIVENESS WOULD BE REQUIRED.

into this scenario, I started praying louder and harder, all day, every day. I wasn't surprised—I was *delighted*—the day she called to ask if I could pick her up for the weekend. I wanted so much to see her and hold her that my immediate response was yes. I would work it out. I would come to get her in the morning.

As soon as I hung up I recognized that the time had come for me to shift out of fear and into a new way of being—*with* him and *for* myself. Healing was at hand, which meant forgiveness would be required. I was willing to forgive him, or so I thought. I called back, got the voice mail, and left a message. I would not be picking my granddaughter up. Instead, I wanted to have a conversation about how we could move forward with less conflict. Five minutes later, he called me back. Two minutes into our conversation, he hung up on me, prompting me to drive to his house.

I had one question I wanted to ask, "What do you want from me?" He had been waiting four years to give me that answer, which he did in a very hushed tone through clenched teeth. I'm not sure what he said, but I was clear that he was hissing at me. It was a warm September day, so I'm not sure why there was a snow shovel on his porch, but there it was, bright and shiny, making itself known to me.

Before I knew what was happening, I had the shovel in my hands and my arms raised up in the air. I was going after him with a vengeance that scared me. Thank God he had the good sense to step backward into his house. As the front door slammed shut in my face, I heard, *"Don't you move! Do not make another move! This is what he needs to prove his point. This will destroy your life."*

I was stunned. I admit that I have played many roles and been many things in my life, but behaving violently is not a hat I have worn. Then again, this day was different. I had an overwhelming need, urge, and/or desire to beat the hell out of something. And after he hissed at me, this man would do just fine. I am grateful that I had equally strong spiritual grounding that let me know I could make another choice.

I dropped the shovel, feeling totally dazed and disoriented. When he opened the door again, the same inner guidance that had adverted the previous potential disaster gave me the next instruction: *"Don't you open your mouth! Turn around and walk away."* I was obedient. Now he was coming after me. I never stopped walking. I could not discern all of what he was saying until he screamed at me, *"You killed Gemmia, and everybody knows it but you!"*

I didn't say a word. I couldn't. Every muscle in my body was convulsing. I am still not sure how I found my keys or sped out of his driveway, spewing gravel in every direction. Racing like a bat out of hell down the quiet streets of the neighborhood, I started praying, *"Have mercy, Lord! Forgive me, Lord! Restore me, Lord! Your grace is my sufficiency! Have mercy, Lord! Forgive me, Lord."* I felt lost. Actually, I was lost. My mind was racing so fast, I didn't recognize where I was and didn't know where I was going. I kept driving and praying until I received my next instruction, *"Remember Lucy."*

Lucy was Gemmia's grandmother, my first husband's mother. I married him as a 19-year-old, guilt-ridden, shame-filled single mother. A month after our wedding, he was deployed to Vietnam. He came back a year later addicted to heroin. After I gave birth to Gemmia, he was arrested for burglarizing his mother's home. He fled New York to avoid prosecution. He had been gone almost three years when I started dating my second husband.

Lucy, my ex-mother-in-law, wanted to remain connected to my children and me. I couldn't even look at her. She represented my past and my past mistakes. I wanted to shut the door on that period of my life, but she had her foot in the door. Now that I was in a new relationship with a man who wanted me and accepted my children, I no longer had a need for her. Rather than have the conversation about how to adjust our relationship, I avoided her, at all costs to her heart and my soul.

> "REMEMBER LUCY. . . ."
> SHE REPRESENTED
> MY PAST AND
> MY PAST MISTAKES.

When Lucy would call, I was short, curt, and always busy. Although she never missed a birthday, Mother's Day, or Christmas, I always had excuses for not bringing the children to visit and for not inviting her to visit them. As horrifying as it was to admit to myself, I had done to her exactly what I judged that my granddaughter's father was now doing to me by withholding my granddaughter.

> THERE IS NO SEPARATION . . . WHEN YOU FIND YOURSELF DOING WHAT SOMEONE ELSE HAS DONE TO YOU, FORGIVENESS DRIVES YOU HEADFIRST INTO PEACEFUL FREEDOM.

I represented his past and his relationship with Gemmia, which had not ended well. He was married to another woman now, with other children of his own. In my mind, that had no bearing whatsoever on my relationship with my granddaughter. As I replayed the shovel scenario over and over, I realized that I was now sitting on the other side of the problem. I was now the grandmother longing to be connected to her grandchild, feeling hurt, dismissed, and disrespected for what seemed like no good reason.

All of a sudden I was filled with enormous compassion for Lucy. I felt her hurt, her sadness, and my own shame. I was barely able to contain my grief as I realized what had happened and what was happening. The best I could do for myself was pull over to the side of the road, weep, and call my best friend Shaheerah. I knew she would walk me through the next moments, hours, or however long it would take for me to digest and understand what was going on. Shaheerah would understand. She would not judge me. Nor would she let me get away with any form of denial. I knew what I had to do because I knew that when you find yourself doing to someone else what was done to you, forgiveness drives you headfirst into peaceful freedom. Lord, did I want to be free.

Forgiving myself was the only way I could get out of the ditch on the side of the road and take myself home. I forgave myself for every judgment I had held about Lucy and my granddaughter's father. I forgave myself for marrying Gemmia's father from a place of fear and perceived desperation. I forgave myself for not forgiving myself for being a teenage mother.

In the flash of a moment, I realized that there is no separation. Life is truly circular. What goes around really does come around. Our work, the really hard work, is to recognize when something huge lands at our front door. Forgiveness opens our mind and heart so that we can recognize the healing opportunity when it shows up. The four years of fighting with my granddaughter's father had nothing to do with him. He was just being himself, living his life in a way that felt right for him. Perhaps one day, his lesson will show up, and he will experience a shift.

My work was to recognize and be willing to tell myself the truth about my own behavior so that I could forgive my past and my current thoughts, beliefs, judgments, and behaviors. Once I was able do that, I drove home and went to bed. There was nothing else I could say or do. There are some aspects of personal healing and spiritual development that are simply exhausting. Forgiving yourself is one of them.

FORGIVENESS OPENS OUR MIND AND HEART

SO THAT WE CAN RECOGNIZE

THE HEALING OPPORTUNITY

WHEN IT SHOWS UP.

DAILY FORGIVENESS PROCESS GUIDELINES

1. **Find a quiet place** where you will not be disturbed for at least 30 to 60 minutes. You can do this work in the morning or just before going to bed. I prefer going through the process at night so I can sleep off any memories that rise to the surface.

2. **Begin by stilling your mind** for at least 5 minutes. You will find the *Stillness Meditation* on the accompanying audio program to be a great support.

3. **Listen to the day's Forgiveness Prayer** on the accompanying audio program. Then read the Forgiveness Prayer offered with the day's practice twice, once silently and once aloud. Hearing the prayer will align you with the Holy Spirit, as it is the presence of the Creator that responds to our slightest request.

4. **Remember to scan the Emotional Triggers List** on pages 9–14, which will prepare you to dig deep into your consciousness. Give yourself permission to be radically honest with yourself about yourself.

5. **Using your journal, write and complete each of the 12 Forgiveness Statements.** Each time you write a Forgiveness Statement, fill in the

blank with your most heartfelt thought or memory to access your innermost thoughts and beliefs.

6. **Perform your Pro EFT^{TM} Forgiveness Tapping Sequences.** Review the general instructions on Tapping into Forgiveness on pages 23–34, then use your own Forgiveness Statements for the day's topic and tap on each of the 10 points outlined on the tapping diagram. If you need additional support, watch the Tapping Videos at www.ProEFT.com.

7. **Process your thoughts and feelings consciously.** As you move through the Tapping into Forgiveness practice, give yourself permission and time to experience any emotions or thoughts that may rise to the surface. Record your additional insights and breakthroughs in your Forgiveness Journal. If at any time you feel overwhelmed, listen to the *Stillness Meditation* again before attempting to complete your practice.

8. **Listen to the *Gratitude Meditation* on the accompanying audio program,** as it will help to restore your mind and heart to balance.

9. **Complete the day's practice** by spending 5 to 10 minutes in quiet reflection or listen to gentle, meditative music.

10. **Be sure to do something good for yourself today.** While you're doing your forgiveness work, remember to be gentle with yourself. Forgiveness doesn't have to be hard or bring you pain. Always keep yourself grounded, be open and willing to receive the healing that's available, and never forget the power of gratitude.

I FORGIVE MYSELF FOR JUDGING MYSELF

Today's Forgiveness Practice is all about forgiving YOU. This is by far the most self-loving, self-honoring, self-affirming gift you can offer yourself. It is the logical place to start because self-forgiveness opens the heart and the mind to greater possibilities. In addition, not until you have forgiven yourself will you have the courage and compassion to forgive anyone else. You cannot *unsee* what you have seen. You cannot *unhear* what you have heard. What you can do, however, is stop wishing that what *has* happened had not happened. For this reason, I think of forgiveness as a "spiritual laxative"—it eliminates long-held mental and emotional toxins.

Regardless of how bad, wrong, or unforgivable you or your behavior has been, you deserve to be and can be forgiven. No matter how hard, challenging, frightening, unjust, or difficult an experience may seem, self-forgiveness is the path to recognizing that everything is just as it needs to be and was just as it needed to be in order for us to heal, grow, and learn. That's just the way the universe works.

A Prayer of Forgiveness

Precious and Beloved God, My Source, and My Creator:

Today, I ask for and open myself to receive the strength, courage, and compassion required to forgive myself. I forgive myself for all perceived sins, faults, mistakes, and failings. I forgive myself for every thought, belief, behavior, perception, and emotion that I have told myself is bad, wrong, unjust, unloving, and displeasing to You, God. I forgive myself for every hurt, judgment, condemnation, unkind or unloving thought, belief, and perception I have held about or against myself. I forgive myself for any behaviors, habits, or actions motivated by unforgiveness, the unwillingness to forgive myself. I forgive myself with compassion and love. I ask for, accept, and claim God's forgiveness. Today, believing and knowing that because I have asked, I have received. I am so grateful.

I let it be!

And so it is!

THE FORGIVENESS

DAY 1
JOURNAL WORK

I FORGIVE
MYSELF

– I Forgive My Mind for Thinking –

EXAMPLE

I forgive my mind for thinking that I always have to do more to prove myself to others.

I forgive my mind for thinking I should be

_____

_____

I forgive my mind for thinking I should not be

_____

_____

I forgive my mind for thinking I am

_____

_____

I forgive my mind for thinking I am not

_____

_____

– I Forgive Myself for Judging –

EXAMPLE

I forgive myself for judging myself as being so stupid about the men I have loved.

I forgive myself for judging myself as

_____

_____

I forgive myself for judging myself as not

_____

_____

I forgive myself for judging myself for

_____

_____

I forgive myself for judging myself for not

_____

_____

– I Forgive Myself for Believing –

EXAMPLE

I forgive myself for believing that all the mean things my grandmother said about me were true.

I forgive myself for believing myself to be

_____

_____

I forgive myself for not believing myself to be

_____

_____

I forgive myself for believing that

_____

_____

I forgive myself for not believing that

_____

_____

– TAPPING SEQUENCE –

BONUS TAPPING SCRIPTS

There are three bonus Tapping Scripts presented during the 21-Day Forgiveness Practice, including "I Forgive Myself," "I Forgive My Mother," and "I Forgive My Relationship with Money." These bonus scripts offer a fascinating glimpse into the intimate inner process of tapping and how people actually use this amazing tool to tackle some of their most challenging problems.

Remember, your forgiveness issues won't necessarily be an identical match with the dialogue presented in the scripts. But the bonus scripts offer examples you can follow for creating your own personalized scripts, drawing from the material in the Forgiveness Statements you created while doing your daily journal work. Customizing the scripts so they reflect your language and clarify your intentions can offer an amazing shortcut to profound personal healing. Remember, the more specific your tapping scripts are, the better your results will be.

BONUS TAPPING SCRIPT DAY 1: "I FORGIVE MYSELF"

IDENTIFY THE ISSUE

The "I Forgive Myself" Bonus Tapping Script deals with the thoughts, judgments, and beliefs we hold about ourselves for past choices and behaviors. After writing out your 12 Forgiveness Statements for Day 1, the specific self-forgiveness issue(s) that you want to work on are becoming increasingly clear. Give the issue a name. Whether you are new to tapping or an old hand, be sure you review Tapping into Forgiveness, on pages 23–34 to refresh your understanding of how the process works. Then you'll be ready to tap into self-forgiveness.

RATE THE INTENSITY LEVEL

On a scale of 0 to 10, where 0 represents "complete freedom from disturbing thoughts" and 10 represents "these thoughts are driving me crazy," rate the intensity of the thoughts, judgments, and beliefs you have about forgiving yourself—for small things to things so large they seem unforgivable.

CLEARING RESISTANCE/THE REVERSAL STATEMENT

The Reversal Statement neutralizes any subconscious resistance you have to releasing your unforgiveness of yourself. It acknowledges your resistance and moves you forward anyway.

Use the Reversal Statement provided below (or one that you've written yourself) and repeat it three times while tapping continuously on the Karate Chop point.

- Even though there is a part of me that is resistant to forgiving myself, even though I say I want to, and then I don't, I deeply and profoundly love and accept myself.

THE SET-UP STATEMENT

The Set-Up Statement helps you stay focused on the issue that you'll be addressing during your tapping session.

Use the Set-Up Statement that follows (or use one that you've written yourself) and repeat it three times while tapping continuously on the Karate Chop point.

- Even though I need to forgive myself, I want to forgive myself, and I have a divine opportunity to forgive myself, I still don't believe I deserve to be forgiven. Yet, I deeply and profoundly love and accept myself.

Shake your hands out and have a few sips of water. Take a deep breath in through your nose. Release the breath slowly and softly through your mouth, making the sound "Ahhhhh" as you do so.

TAPPING SEQUENCE: ROUNDS 1 THROUGH 3

For Tapping Rounds 1 through 3, tap 7 times on each of the 10 meridian points while repeating the Tapping Script that follows, or create your own script using the Forgiveness Statement entries from your daily journal work as your reminder phrases. Using your own personal Forgiveness Statements will keep you laser focused on your tapping intention as different dimensions of your healing process unfold.

ROUND I

Tap 7 times on each meridian point while repeating out loud either the statements below or your reminder phrases.

Eyebrow:	I feel guilty and ashamed about some of the things that I've thought, said, and done.
Side of Eye:	And the way that I have hurt myself and other people.
Under Eye:	I feel so guilty about some things I have done and not done.
Under Nose:	I feel so ashamed about certain things I have said and done.
Chin:	I feel embarrassed about things I have said and done or not said and not done.
Collarbone:	Someplace inside of me, it feels as if I am not a very nice person or a good person.
Underarm:	I feel as if I'm not even worth forgiving.
Liver:	I am learning how to forgive other people, but I can't seem to forgive myself.
Wrists:	I am carrying around so much unforgiveness.
Crown of Head:	I feel so bad about myself, so unforgiving.

ROUND 2

Tap 7 times on each meridian point while repeating out loud either the statements below or your reminder phrases.

Eyebrow:	What if I stop beating myself up?
Side of Eye:	What if it's time to start letting go of the guilt, shame, and unforgiveness?
Under Eye:	What if I acknowledge that everything is a lesson and that I was just doing the best I could?
Under Nose:	What if I let go of the feeling that I can't forgive myself?
Chin:	What if making that small choice starts the forgiveness process?
Collarbone:	What if I forgive myself a little at a time so that I feel safe and comfortable?
Underarm:	What if I release all feelings of guilt, shame, and blame?
Liver:	What if I give myself permission to transform my unforgive-ness and self-judgment into peace and freedom?
Wrists:	What if nothing happens?
Crown of Head:	What if something does happen, something like I forgive myself?

ROUND 3

Tap 7 times on each meridian point while repeating out loud either the statements below or your reminder phrases.

Eyebrow:	It feels as if I am ready to release all forms of unforgiveness toward myself.
Side of Eye:	It feels like I am opening to the possibility of forgiving myself totally and completely.
Under Eye:	It feels like I am already forgiven by everyone for everything.
Under Nose:	This forgiveness is very powerful.
Chin:	I am tapping into the power of forgiveness right now.
Collarbone:	I am much more open and much better now.
Underarm:	I am open to forgiving myself for creating or choosing experiences that require self-forgiveness.
Liver:	I have learned my lessons and release the need to repeat them.
Wrists:	I allow my mind and heart to experience total and complete forgiveness of myself for everything.
Crown of Head:	I know that everything has happened for my highest and greatest good. Thank you! Thank you! Thank you!

Have a few sips of water. Take a deep breath in through your nose. Release the breath slowly and softly through your mouth, making the sound "Ahhhhh" as you do so.

RECHECK THE INTENSITY LEVEL

Recheck your intensity level on holding unforgiveness about yourself. If the level is at 8 or higher, repeat the entire 3-Round Tapping Sequence outlined in the bonus Tapping Script (or your self-created script.)

If the level is less than 8, tap on one of the following Modified Set-Up Statements, then perform the 10-point Tapping Sequence on the 12 Forgiveness Statements from your daily journal work.

MODIFIED SET-UP STATEMENT

Use the Modified Set-Up Statement below (or use one that you've written yourself) and repeat it three times while tapping continuously on the Karate Chop point.

- Even though I still have some stubborn judgments about myself and some resistance to letting them go, I am willing to let them go, and I love and accept myself totally and unconditionally.

After you complete the Tapping Sequence on your Forgiveness Statements, recheck your intensity level on holding unforgiveness about yourself.

Depending on your level, continue to repeat the sequence described above until you are at a 0 level of intensity.

– REFLECTIONS –

I have learned that the person I have to ask for forgiveness from the most is: myself. You must love yourself. You have to forgive yourself, every day. . . . Because that's what love is like.

— C. JOY BELL

I Forgive My Body

My thoughts are images that I have made.

Things that I see
are made of the thoughts I think.

My thoughts create images.
The images I see
reflect the thoughts I am thinking.
I am responsible for what I see.
I can train my mind to be a deliberate
creator of what I see.

—Prayer for *A Course in Miracles Workbook*
Lesson 15

– Forgiveness Story by Iyanla Vanzant –

I grew up believing that I was fat and ugly and that I would always be fat and ugly. I was fat because I believed my grandmother when she told me that I ate too much. I was ugly because I believed my brother when he said I was not in line when God was giving out good looks. By the time I became interested in classical ballet, my distorted body image was signed, sealed, and delivered into the recesses of my mind. In dance class, where all the other dancers had small breasts and hips, I felt out of place. Many of the other prepubescent girls had enough hair to make a lovely ballerina bun on the nape of their necks. I was not so blessed or lucky. Still, I showed up for dance class each day in junior high and high school, believing that every comment the teacher made about points, pirouettes, and grand jetés was directed toward me because I was fat, ugly, and my hair was short.

I was 16 years old when I first saw a performance by Michael Babatunde Olatunji, the master drummer from Nigeria. His dancers looked like me. They were round and limber, and boy could they move. For the first time in my life I understood that I did not need to be thin to be beautiful or to dance. I also recognized that ballet was not the only form of dance available to me, and that I did not need a bun on the nape of my neck to fit into the world of dance. It was my first step toward accepting that God created poodles and S/He also created Saint Bernards. Not everyone needs to be a size 2, and at a size 10, I was by no means fat. The problem was, I had seen myself as fat and ugly for so long, it was difficult for me to imagine myself as anything else. Thank God for the 1960s, when short hair among women of color became fashionable, and round bodies could be covered with a dashiki! The black power fashion trends of the 1960s did not totally eliminate my distorted body image problem, but they certainly took me to the next step—self-acceptance.

Many people have distorted images and beliefs about their bodies that are held in place by a host of unconscious and habitual thoughts or beliefs. Today, these thoughts are called "negative body bashing." They give rise to a host of esteem, worth, and value issues, particularly among women.

There are some schools of thought that promote the concept that the physical body is an "outpicturing" of the thoughts and emotions we hold about who we are and where our place is in the world. Other schools believe that if you don't follow a specific dietary

> IF YOU THINK YOU ARE FAT OR NEED TO BE FAT, YOUR BODY WILL ACCOMMODATE THOSE THOUGHTS.

and exercise regimen, the body will simply become a reflection of what you are not doing. Then, there is the other reality. Your body is a living organism that hears and believes every thought you think and every word you speak. It follows from this particular train of thought that nothing goes on in the body that does not first occur in the mind.

If you think you are fat or need to be fat, your body will accommodate those thoughts. If you believe that you are just fine as you are, then you will live accordingly, whether or not those thoughts are productive and supportive for your health and well-being. The issue here is not whether you are a size 2 or size 22. The issue is, What do you believe about your body? And what thoughts are you feeding yourself consciously and unconsciously?

Mental images determine how we behave when confronted by daily life experiences. If we think of ourselves as worthwhile and valued, it will come across to other people and we will be treated accordingly. When, on the other hand, we see ourselves as less than, as not as good as, or in some way as inferior or deficient because of how we look, we will receive a corresponding reaction from those with whom we interact. Molded by both internal and external influences, self-image and body image can make a huge difference in how we interact with the world.

I was 22 and the mother of three children when my son Damon said, "Mommy, you are the prettiest mommy in the world." He was six years old at the time. I remember it because I was getting dressed to go job hunting. Damon was sitting on the edge of the bed watching me as I tried to get my white blouse to lay flat inside of my black skirt. *Nobody*, I thought to myself, *looks fat or ugly in a white blouse and black skirt.* They look acceptable. They look appropriate and adequate and beautiful. They look employable. More important, they are pretty.

I carried Damon's words with me all day, repeating them over and over as if they were a personal mantra: *I am the prettiest mommy in the world, and I am going to get this job.* On the subway, when I caught someone looking at me from the corner of my eye, I thought to myself, *They are looking at me because I am pretty.*

The interview went smoothly, although I did not get the job. Didn't matter. On that day, my historical programming of being fat and ugly was overwritten by a new thought. I became the prettiest mommy in the world for my son, and I have been that way ever since; even now, at a size 12, with my choice to keep my hair short and to eat all the chicken wings I can get my hands on.

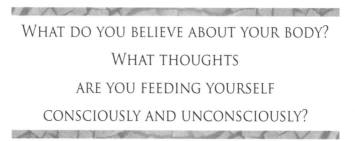

WHAT DO YOU BELIEVE ABOUT YOUR BODY?

WHAT THOUGHTS

ARE YOU FEEDING YOURSELF

CONSCIOUSLY AND UNCONSCIOUSLY?

DAILY FORGIVENESS
PROCESS REMINDERS

For a more detailed explanation
of the Daily Forgiveness Process Guidelines, see pages 45–46.

1. Find a quiet place where you will not be disturbed for at least 30 to 60 minutes.

2. Still your mind for at least 5 minutes or listen to the *Stillness Meditation*.

3. Listen to the *Forgiveness Prayer* on the accompanying audio program. Then read the Forgiveness Prayer, once silently and once aloud.

4. Scan the Emotional Trigger List on pages 9–14.

5. Write out the 12 Forgiveness Statements for each day's topic on thinking, judging, and believing in your Forgiveness Journal (Days 1–18). Write your Forgiveness Letters (Days 19–21).

6. Perform your Pro EFT™ Forgiveness Tapping Sequences.

7. Process thoughts and feelings consciously through your Forgiveness Journal Reflections.

8. Listen to the *Gratitude Meditation*.

9. Complete the day's practice in quiet reflection or with meditative music.

10. Be sure to do something good for yourself today!

I Forgive Myself for Judging My Body

Today's Forgiveness Practice is all about forgiving the beliefs and distorted images you may have about your body. Is your perception of your body giving you low self-esteem? Is it difficult for you to receive compliments about how you look? Do your friends and family members see you differently than you see yourself? Do you avoid certain situations because you feel out of place? Are you constantly criticizing and judging your physical features? Body size? Body structure?

We have all at one time or another compared ourselves to others we believe are better looking or in better shape than we consider ourselves to be in. Again, the issue here is not how big or small you are. The issue is eliminating the habitual, negative, and destructive thoughts or beliefs you may be holding about your body that impact your self-esteem, worth, and value.

In many cases what we have come to believe about our bodies is a function of what we have been told or not told.

A Prayer of Forgiveness

Dear God:

Today, I ask for and open myself to receive a new image of myself. I recognize that in Your eyes, I am perfect as I am. I understand that if there is anything about my body that I choose to change, You have empowered me to do so. I have the power of free will. I have the power of choice. Today, I am choosing to change how I see myself, change how I speak to myself, change how I present myself to the world. I am choosing to see myself as You see me. I am choosing to surrender, release, and heal all negative, toxic, unloving thoughts about my body and to accept myself as Your beautiful creation. I ask, if there is anything within me that is not pleasing to You, that it be lifted. I ask that all habitual, unconscious thoughts, beliefs, and memories about my body be brought into alignment with Your thoughts, beliefs, and plans for me. I ask for the strength and courage to make any changes that are required so that I will accept myself, honor myself, and love myself as You do.

I let it be!

And so it is!

THE FORGIVENESS

DAY 2
JOURNAL WORK

---

*I FORGIVE
MY BODY*

– I Forgive My Mind for Thinking –

EXAMPLE

I forgive my mind for thinking my body is ugly/dirty/distorted/useless/ too large, etc.

I forgive my mind for thinking my body is

_____

_____

I forgive my mind for thinking my body is not

_____

_____

I forgive my mind for thinking my body should be

_____

_____

I forgive my mind for thinking my body should not be

_____

_____

– I Forgive Myself for Judging –

EXAMPLE

I forgive myself for judging my body as embarrassing because it is larger than my sister's body.

I forgive myself for judging my body as

_____

_____

I forgive myself for judging my body as

_____

_____

I forgive myself for judging my body as

_____

_____

I forgive myself for judging my body as

_____

_____

– I Forgive Myself for Believing –

EXAMPLE

I forgive myself for believing that my body is fat and that I am ugly.

I forgive myself for believing _____

_____

I forgive myself for believing _____

_____

I forgive myself for believing _____

_____

I forgive myself for believing _____

_____

– TAPPING SEQUENCE –

Review Basic Tapping Sequence Guidelines on pages 53–59.

1. Review each of the day's 12 Forgiveness Statements out loud. This will help you identify the specific aspects of the issue that you want to tap on.

2. Rate the intensity level of any unforgiveness you hold about today's topic on a scale of 1 to 10. Write the number down.

3. Neutralize all subconscious resistance. Repeat a Reversal Statement 3 times while tapping continuously on the Karate Chop point.

4. Focus on the issue you'll be tapping on. Repeat a Set-Up Statement 3 times while tapping continuously on the Karate Chop point.

5. Tap 7 times on each of the 10 meridian points while repeating out loud the key details from the 12 Forgiveness Statements. This process can be modeled on the bonus Tapping Scripts.

6. Recheck the intensity level of any unforgiveness you hold about today's topic. Write the number down. If the level is at 8 or higher, repeat the entire sequence. If the level is less than 8, tap on a Modified Set-Up Statement, then perform the 10-point Tapping Sequence on your 12 Forgiveness Statements until you are at a 0 level of intensity.

– REFLECTIONS –

_____

_____

_____

_____

_____

_____

_____

_____

_____

_____

_____

_____

_____

Few suffer more than those who refuse to forgive themselves.

— MIKE NORTON, *FIGHTING FOR REDEMPTION*

I FORGIVE MY LIFE

Your grace is given me. I claim it now.

Your grace is given me.
I claim it now.

"Ask, and it is given.
You deny me nothing.
If I have not, it is because I ask not."

—PRAYER FOR *A COURSE IN MIRACLES WORKBOOK*
LESSON 168

– Forgiveness Story by Iyanla Vanzant –

The good thing about taking a workshop is that you get to do the work. A really good workshop will provide you with the information, tools, and process required to address the issue that is the topic of the workshop. An excellent workshop is one that will provide you with the information, tools, and process required to address whatever the topic is—and then challenge you do to the work right then and there.

I was attending an excellent workshop. The topic of the excellent workshop was Learning How to Fly . . . Beyond Self-Imposed Limitations. The Unity Church in downtown Philadelphia was hosting it. The cost was $450.00 for the six-day process, and I did not have the money.

When I decided to leave my position with the Philadelphia public defender's office, I had no clue what I wanted to do with my life. I was 36 years old at the time, and I had been working steadily since the age of 13. I graduated from college when I was 33, left my hometown of New York, and moved to Pennsylvania to begin what I thought would be the rest of my life. Practicing criminal law, saving people from the pitfalls of the judicial system, and changing the world were the only things on my to-do list.

When I realized that I was not cut out to spend the rest of my life going in and out of penal institutions and courtrooms, it felt as if I had hit a very large, very hard brick wall. I was in a new city, alone after ending a long-term relationship. I had two children and a cat to feed, plus a very large student-loan bill. I had no vision, no interests, no desires, and no clue about what to do next to support my family and myself.

But wait! I had a college degree. I consider myself fairly intelligent. Actually, I was smart enough to complete my undergraduate degree with a 3.99 GPA. I had some pretty decent work experience. I had worked in retail sales, publishing, advertising, and law. I also had experiences with welfare, homelessness, poverty, domestic abuse, and my drug of choice—unworthiness.

Guess which experiences loomed in the forefront of my mind? Need I say anything more? With all that I had overcome and accomplished, I found myself paralyzed by fear of failure, anticipation of rejection, hopelessness, and my grandmother's theme song for my life, "You will never amount to nothin', just like your daddy!" When I came across the advertisement for the workshop, I knew it was the answer to a prayer that I had yet to pray.

When I called the church to inquire about registering for the workshop, I had no idea it had a price tag attached to it. I guess I just assumed it would be free. It was a false assumption.

"We will begin at 6 p.m. Friday. We will meet from 9 a.m. until 9 p.m. on Saturday. We will meet from noon until 9 p.m. on Sunday. We will meet from 6 p.m. until 10 p.m. next Monday through Friday and again from 9 a.m. until 9 p.m. next Saturday. Are you still interested?"

"Absolutely."

"Great! How would you like to pay your registration fee?"

"Oh! I'm not sure. How much is it?"

"Four hundred and fifty dollars. We accept cash, checks, and credit cards."

It was then that I knew this was going to be an excellent workshop and that I needed to start praying. I told the lovely woman I would get back to her.

It is not until your back is against the wall that you discover things about your character. I was a fighter. In this case, I was fighting for my life and a way to move it forward. I knew that I was very resourceful. I had raised three children without much support from their fathers, and none of us were hungry or naked. I also knew that I had a very limiting tendency to believe that I could not have what I wanted, so why bother asking. With this awareness, I shifted from fight mode to surrender and began to pray. I don't remember what I prayed for, but I do remember what I prayed about. I prayed for guidance and direction. I prayed for forgiveness of everything I believed about myself and my life that was untrue or unloving or useless. I prayed the words of the 23rd Psalm because that was my fail-safe prayer. I prayed the words of the 27th Psalm because that was my lift-me-from-this-mess prayer. I prayed the 91st Psalm because I knew it by heart, and then I wept and prayed, "Dear God, help me." Weeping may endure for a night but joy cometh when you stop weeping.

I called the church and asked to speak to the registrar. Without a moment of hesitation, I made my plea.

"I am asking for grace to pay for this workshop on a payment plan. I receive $265 each week in unemployment benefits. I can pay a portion of that every week for the next four weeks until the balance is paid in full."

The space between us was so still, I wasn't sure she had heard me. When she spoke, I couldn't believe my ears.

"I do not have the authority to make that type of arrangement. The full amount of the registration fee is due on or before the last day of class. That will be next Saturday at 9 p.m. Do I have your commitment that you will honor this arrangement?"

Without thinking I said, "Yes." In that moment, the workshop began for me.

I did not know how or from where the money would come, but I knew it would come. Every morning as soon as my feet hit the floor, I prayed the same prayers. I went to each class day without giving a thought to how I would pay for my participation.

> I HAD A VERY LIMITING TENDENCY TO BELIEVE THAT I COULD NOT HAVE WHAT I WANTED, SO WHY BOTHER ASKING.

During the Wednesday evening class, the facilitator challenged me about who I was choosing to be. He asked me for a 25-word statement to the universe of life as a declaration of how I planned to show up in the world from that day forward. As the only person of color in the room, I was a bit hesitant to declare myself as anything. All of the issues related to being not good enough, inferior, less than, and unimportant that had been laying dormant in my consciousness stood at full attention and held my mouth glued shut. The facilitator asked me if I intended to remain not good enough, inferior, less than everyone one else, and unimportant in order to hide the gifts God has given me. Waves of shock and horrification flooded every fiber of my being, and I suddenly became faint. The facilitator was now barking at me:

"Stand up straight! Open your mouth and honor God, or take your limited mind out of my sight! Who are you choosing to be?"

From somewhere between my big toe and my second toe, the words spilled out of my mouth:

"I used to be just another poor black woman. From this day forth, I choose to be a child of God every day."

"Great!" he said. "That was 23 words." Then he moved on to the next person with a different challenge.

> WHY HAD I PRAYED FOR JUST WHAT I NEEDED RATHER THAN ASKING GOD TO HANDLE EVERYTHING?

When I came home from class Thursday evening, I felt compelled to go through the stack of mail on my desk. I had been avoiding the multicolored envelopes filled with overdue bills. When I saw the brown envelope from the state of Pennsylvania, my heart literally skipped a beat. Methodically moving the letter opener through the tightly sealed flap of the envelope, I removed what I knew was a check. Before I turned it over, I prayed, "Wait on the Lord and be of good courage." Pay to the Order . . . $457, retroactive unemployment benefits.

The limitations of my consciousness were now in full view. Why had I prayed for just what I needed rather than asking God to handle everything?

Daily Forgiveness
Process Reminders

For a more detailed explanation
of the Daily Forgiveness Process Guidelines, see pages 45–46.

1. Find a quiet place where you will not be disturbed for at least 30 to 60 minutes.

2. Still your mind for at least 5 minutes or listen to the *Stillness Meditation*.

3. Listen to the *Forgiveness Prayer* on the accompanying audio program. Then read the Forgiveness Prayer, once silently and once aloud.

4. Scan the Emotional Trigger List on pages 9–14.

5. Write out the 12 Forgiveness Statements for each day's topic on thinking, judging, and believing in your Forgiveness Journal (Days 1–18). Write your Forgiveness Letters (Days 19–21).

6. Perform your Pro EFT™ Forgiveness Tapping Sequences.

7. Process thoughts and feelings consciously through your Forgiveness Journal Reflections.

8. Listen to the *Gratitude Meditation*.

9. Complete the day's practice in quiet reflection or with meditative music.

10. Be sure to do something good for yourself today!

I Forgive Myself for Judging My Life

Today's Forgiveness Practice is about forgiving the judgments and limitations you may be holding about your life. Life is a series of unfolding possibilities, opportunities that are ignited by the choices we make moment to moment. When the consciousness is filled with judgments and fears about what has not happened in response to what has already happened, we limit the greater good that life holds. No matter how many times or how long you have wished, hoped, and prayed for something, because it has not happened yet does not mean it will not happen. Life follows the energy of our focus and faith. If you put your faith in what has not, may not, will not happen, life will deliver more of *that* to your front door—it will not happen.

Another pitfall we humans face is looking at the circumstances and situations of our lives in any given moment and calling it all that is possible. Remember, in my mind, I thought of myself as just another poor black woman. With a college degree, a law degree, and more than 20 years of work experience, I could not see beyond the experience of unemployment. Referencing my historical experiences of being poor and homeless and of feeling unsupported, I was predicting a future that would mirror my past.

Life is about so much more than we can imagine, yet we must give ourselves permission to imagine it if we want to experience it. Forgiving ourselves for the judgments we have held about what did, did not, should have, or should not have happened throughout our life experiences opens mental and emotional space to choose new possibilities. One of my favorite statements from *A Course in Miracles* is: "All things are lessons that God would have us learn." One of the rewards of forgiveness is that it moves us to the head of the class where we can see and recognize the lessons and strengths we have gained from every experience.

LIFE FOLLOWS THE ENERGY OF OUR FOCUS AND FAITH. IF YOU PUT YOUR FAITH IN WHAT HAS NOT, MAY NOT, WILL NOT HAPPEN, LIFE WILL DELIVER MORE OF *THAT* TO YOUR FRONT DOOR—IT WILL NOT HAPPEN.

A Prayer of Forgiveness

Dear and Precious Lord of the Universe:

I now ask that You untie the nots that have invaded my mind, my heart, and my life. I now ask that You remove the have nots, can nots, and do nots that are occupying space in my mind. I now ask that You erase the will nots, may nots, and might nots that invade my heart. I now ask that You release me from the could nots, would nots, and should nots that limit my ability to receive more good than I have ever known.

Most of all my dear God, I now ask that You disintegrate and eliminate all of the am nots from my mind, heart, and life that I have allowed to hold me back from the endless possibilities You have in store for me. Today, dear Father God, I come to You humbly asking that You untie, eliminate, and erase all of the nots that I have chosen to entertain rather than remembering all that You have promised me.

I ask that these words be received in the presence of Your Holy Spirit and become conditions in my life.

I let it be!

And so it is!

—Excerpted from *Every Day I Pray*

THE FORGIVENESS

DAY 3
JOURNAL WORK

*I FORGIVE
MY LIFE*

– I Forgive My Mind for Thinking –

EXAMPLE

I forgive my mind for thinking unproductive thoughts about my life.

I forgive my mind for thinking my life is

_____

_____

I forgive my mind for thinking my life is not

_____

_____

I forgive my mind for thinking my life should

_____

_____

I forgive my mind for thinking my life should not

_____

_____

– I FORGIVE MYSELF FOR JUDGING –

EXAMPLE

I forgive myself for judging my life as useless and hopeless as it is right now.

I forgive myself for judging my life as

_____

_____

I forgive myself for judging my life as

_____

_____

I forgive myself for judging my life as

_____

_____

I forgive myself for judging my life as

_____

_____

– I Forgive Myself for Believing –

EXAMPLE

I forgive myself for believing my life is a mess.

I forgive myself for believing my life is/is not

_____

_____

I forgive myself for believing my life should/should not

_____

_____

I forgive myself for believing my life may never

_____

_____

I forgive myself for believing my life will always

_____

_____

– TAPPING SEQUENCE –

Review Basic Tapping Sequence Guidelines on pages 53–59.

1. Review each of the day's 12 Forgiveness Statements out loud. This will help you identify the specific aspects of the issue that you want to tap on.

2. Rate the intensity level of any unforgiveness you hold about today's topic on a scale of 1 to 10. Write the number down.

3. Neutralize all subconscious resistance. Repeat a Reversal Statement 3 times while tapping continuously on the Karate Chop point.

4. Focus on the issue you'll be tapping on. Repeat a Set-Up Statement 3 times while tapping continuously on the Karate Chop point.

5. Tap 7 times on each of the 10 meridian points while repeating out loud the key details from the 12 Forgiveness Statements. This process can be modeled on the bonus Tapping Scripts.

6. Recheck the intensity level of any unforgiveness you hold about today's topic. Write the number down. If the level is at 8 or higher, repeat the entire sequence. If the level is less than 8, tap on a Modified Set-Up Statement, then perform the 10-point Tapping Sequence on your 12 Forgiveness Statements until you are at a 0 level of intensity.

_____

_____

_____

_____

_____

_____

_____

_____

_____

_____

_____

Forgiving does not erase the bitter past. A healed memory
is not a deleted memory. Instead, forgiving what we
cannot forget creates a new way to remember.
We change the memory of our past into a hope for our future.

— LEWIS B. SMEDES

I Forgive My Mother

I do not know what anything is for.
Everything is for my own best interests.

God created no opposites, nothing that
attacks, no-thing that could harm,
obstruct, or obscure love's presence.
If I am seeing something that is blocking
my awareness of love, it is an image
of a false idea that I created and only
forgiveness will dissolve it.

—Prayer for *A Course in Miracles Workbook*
Lesson 25

– Forgiveness Story by Iyanla Vanzant –

I didn't know my mother. I wish I had, but when she passed on, I was two and a half, and the big people in charge thought it best not to tell me. I was 30 when I discovered that the woman I was raised to believe was mother was in fact my stepmother. She had married my father three years before I was born.

My mother was "the other woman" in my father's life. I loved my stepmother dearly, but she could not fill the vacancy in my soul left by my mother's departure. Once I knew the truth, pieces and parts of my life made much more sense.

Growing up, I was always in awe of the relationship between my friends and their mothers. Living with my aunt as a family foster child, I always yearned for "my mother" to be there and do the things that I saw my friends doing with their mothers. In fact, I remember being quite disturbed, sometimes angry, when my friends spoke ill of their mothers. The normal mother-daughter squabbles took on an entirely different meaning in my heart and mind. Somewhere deep inside of me, without words or sound, I knew that to have your mother in your life was a blessing. My aunt did the best she could for as long as she could, but I was not her child. When my father and stepmother sent my brother and me to live with her, it was like a double whammy. My mother, who wasn't really my mother, was gone, compounding the unspoken yearning I had for my natural mother, whom I hardly knew and didn't remember. *Oh Lord! What a hot mess!*

I used to always say that I was not a good mother. I was a great provider and rigorous disciplinarian, both of which made me a horrible mother. I can say that about myself now because I have learned the true role and function of a mother in a child's life. In fact, my name, *Iyanla,* means *great mother.* It is more than a name. In the cultures of many West African villages, the *Iyanla* is the eldest woman in the village who has the responsibility to provide for the spiritual well-being of the community. As such, fulfilling the duties of the title is something that I have grown into and learned with much prayer and great study. As a function of life, "great mother" is not, I'm sure, what my children experienced, nor is it what they needed or expected from their mommy.

> A MOTHER IS HER CHILDREN'S FIRST TEACHER. HER RELATIONSHIP WITH HER CHILDREN BEGINS WHEN THEY ARE IN THE WOMB.

A mother is her children's first teacher. Her relationship with her children begins when they are in the womb. How a woman thinks about, cares for, and nourishes her own being mentally, emotionally, physically, and spiritually sends powerful and important messages into the fabric of her children. What a mother thinks sends impulses into her children's minds. What she says sends vibrational energy into her children's hearts. What she does and how she does it creates the expectations her children will have for themselves, within themselves. The depth of a mother's involvement with and her relationship to her children is unique and different because of the strong emotional and physical bonding that has occurred. How she bonds and whether or not she bonds teaches her children what they can expect from the most important relationships they will have in life.

I once read a fable that made it very clear to me that my purpose as a mother went way beyond provision and discipline:

One day in a busy marketplace, a mother bumped into a stranger as he tried to pass. "Oh! Please excuse me. I wasn't paying attention and did not see you." The stranger said, "Please excuse me, too, for I am as guilty as you for not paying attention." Both the stranger and the mother were very polite and laughed lightly as they walked their separate ways.

Later that day the mother was at home preparing the evening meal for her family. Her son came into the kitchen unnoticed by his mother and stood beside her. When she turned around, she nearly tripped over him and knocked him to the floor. "Move out of the way," she yelled at him. "I'm busy now. Leave me alone." With his heart broken, the child walked away, going into his room, where he cried. The busy mother had not realized how harshly she had spoken to him. Nor did she recognize the gift that had been in his hand.

Later that night the mother lay awake in her bed reviewing in her mind the events of the day. When she closed her eyes to whisper her nightly prayer, a small voice whispered into her ears, "While dealing with a stranger, you were polite and courteous, yet when it came to the child you say you love, you chose harsh impatience. Go back into the kitchen. Look in the corner by the door. There you will find the flowers your son picked for you. He stood quietly in the kitchen waiting to surprise you. What you offered to the stranger is the very least of what you son deserves from you, his mother." The mother shot upright in her bed. Untangling herself from her bedcovers, she did as directed. Sure enough, she found the flowers.

Now, she wept. She quietly went and knelt at the side of her son's bed, not wanting to disturb him. There she prayed, "Dear God, please forgive me for the way I treated our son today. I confess that I yelled at him and caused him pain. I confess that I allowed what I had to do to be more important than being the mother You created me to be. Please God, forgive me and teach me to love my children the way You do."

Children need a mother's love, acceptance, and nurturing, particularly when they least deserve it. A mother must be aware that if she were to die tomorrow, the children she leaves behind will experience the loss of her presence for the rest of their lives. It is not uncommon for a mother to fall short of the importance of her role. Yet it is essential for her to recognize these shortcomings and be willing to make amends within herself, with God, and with her children. It also goes without saying that before a woman becomes a mother, she is a woman with patterns and pathologies to be healed, needs and desires to be fulfilled, lessons to learn, and a life's purpose to fulfill. What I have learned about being a woman with a purpose and a mother by divine design is that the only way I will experience peace, joy, and fulfillment as a wife and mother is to create and maintain an intimate relationship with God. When that was not in place, I was left to my own devices. Just ask my children.

Daily Forgiveness Process Reminders

For a more detailed explanation
of the Daily Forgiveness Process Guidelines, see pages 45–46.

1. Find a quiet place where you will not be disturbed for at least 30 to 60 minutes.

2. Still your mind for at least 5 minutes or listen to the *Stillness Meditation.*

3. Listen to the *Forgiveness Prayer* on the accompanying audio program. Then read the Forgiveness Prayer, once silently and once aloud.

4. Scan the Emotional Trigger List on pages 9–14.

5. Write out the 12 Forgiveness Statements for each day's topic on thinking, judging, and believing in your Forgiveness Journal (Days 1–18). Write your Forgiveness Letters (Days 19–21).

6. Perform your Pro EFT™ Forgiveness Tapping Sequences.

7. Process thoughts and feelings consciously through your Forgiveness Journal Reflections.

8. Listen to the *Gratitude Meditation.*

9. Complete the day's practice in quiet reflection or with meditative music.

10. Be sure to do something good for yourself today!

I FORGIVE MYSELF FOR JUDGING MY MOTHER

Today's Forgiveness Practice is about forgiving the judgments, hurts, and wounds that may be buried in your consciousness and are engraved into your mother's name. You will be forgiving all thoughts, beliefs, memories, and experiences you may have judged as wrong, unfair, unkind, or unloving. This does not mean that your experience of your mother is wrong or that her behavior was right or appropriate. The process of forgiveness is designed to neutralize what is going on within you in order to make space for another possibility to unfold. Regardless of how you hold her in consciousness, your mother represents the very beating of your heart, because her heartbeat was the first sound you heard. To forgive your mother opens and heals your heart.

> YOUR MOTHER REPRESENTS THE VERY BEATING OF YOUR HEART.

Be sure to reread pages 15–22 in order to gain clarity about how your thoughts and judgments can become the feelings you may have about your mother.

A PRAYER OF FORGIVENESS

Blessed Father God, Holy Mother God:

Today, I ask for and allow myself to receive and experience Your grace. Today, I claim my freedom as I declare my willingness and readiness to release my mother from all of my anger, hurt, woundedness, judgment, disappointment, and sorrow hidden anywhere in my consciousness or being. I surrender all memories, experiences, circumstances, and situations where I have held my mother with blame or fault. I ask to be lifted above any and all judgments, critiques, assessments, perceptions, beliefs, and habitual patterns of thought in which I see and hold my mother as anything less than Your perfect child. I ask that You fill me with Your compassion, Your truth, Your knowledge that allows me to see my mother as Your daughter whom You love and in whom You are well pleased. Lift me beyond my intellect and ego that I may behold my mother with all my heart as You do.

I rest in Thee.

I let it be!

And so it is!

THE FORGIVENESS

DAY 4
JOURNAL WORK

---

*I Forgive
My Mother*

– I Forgive My Mind for Thinking –

EXAMPLE

I forgive my mind for thinking my mother was more loving to my sister/brother than she was toward me.

I forgive my mind for thinking my mother was

_____

_____

I forgive my mind for thinking my mother was not

_____

_____

I forgive my mind for thinking my mother should have

_____

_____

I forgive my mind for thinking my mother should not have

_____

_____

– I Forgive Myself for Judging –

EXAMPLE

I forgive myself for judging my mother for divorcing my father.

I forgive myself for judging my mother for

_____

_____

I forgive myself for judging my mother for not

_____

_____

I forgive myself for judging my mother about

_____

_____

I forgive myself for judging my mother when

_____

_____

– I Forgive Myself for Believing –

EXAMPLE

I forgive myself for believing my mother made me feel stupid.

I forgive myself for believing my mother made me feel

_____

_____

I forgive myself for believing my mother did not make me feel

_____

_____

I forgive myself for believing my mother should not have made me feel

_____

_____

I forgive myself for believing my mother should have made me feel

_____

_____

– TAPPING SEQUENCE –

BONUS TAPPING SCRIPT DAY 4: "I FORGIVE MY MOTHER"

IDENTIFY THE ISSUE AND RATE THE INTENSITY LEVEL

After writing out your 12 Forgiveness Statements for Day 4, the specific mother forgiveness issue(s) that you want to work on are becoming increasingly clear. Give the issue a name. Now on a scale of 0 to 10, where 0 represents "complete freedom from disturbing thoughts" and 10 represents "these thoughts are driving me crazy," rate the intensity of the thoughts, judgments, and beliefs you have about your "unforgiveness" of your mother.

CLEARING RESISTANCE/THE REVERSAL STATEMENT

The Reversal Statement neutralizes any subconscious resistance you have to releasing your unforgiveness of your mother. It acknowledges your resistance and moves you forward anyway.

Use the Reversal Statement provided below (or one that you've written yourself) and repeat it three times while tapping continuously on the Karate Chop point.

- Even though there is a part of me that is resistant to forgiving my mother, and no one can make me change my mind, I deeply and profoundly love and accept myself.

Shake your hands out and have a few sips of water. Take a deep breath in through your nose. Release the breath slowly and softly through your mouth, making the sound "Ahhhhh" as you do so.

THE SET-UP STATEMENT

The Set-Up Statement helps you focus on the issue that you'll be addressing during your tapping session. Choose one of the Set-Up Statements below (or use one that you've written yourself) and repeat it three times while tapping continuously on the Karate Chop point.

- Even though I have all of this pent-up unforgiveness toward my mother, I have a right to be angry for the way she treated me. I refuse to let it go, because it is my anger, my resentment, my bitterness, and I still love myself and respect my feelings.

- Even though there is a part of me that believes that my mother has no right to expect my forgiveness, I sometimes want to let her off the hook for some of the horrible things she has done, but I can't. Nevertheless, I still deeply and profoundly love and accept myself.

- Even though withholding my forgiveness is keeping me stuck in anger at my mother, there's a part of me that doesn't want to let it go. I want to love and accept myself anyway.

Shake your hands out and have a few sips of water. Take a deep breath in through your nose. Release the breath slowly and softly through your mouth, making the sound "Ahhhhh" as you do so.

TAPPING SEQUENCE: ROUNDS 1 THROUGH 3

For Tapping Rounds 1 through 3, tap 7 times on each of the 10 meridian points while repeating the Tapping Script that follows, or create your own script using the Forgiveness Statement entries from your daily journal work as reminder phrases. Using your own personal Forgiveness Statements will keep you laser-focused on your tapping intention as different dimensions of your healing process unfold.

ROUND I

Tap 7 times on each meridian point while repeating out loud either the statements below or your reminder phrases.

Eyebrow:	I feel really, really angry with my mother.
Side of Eye:	I feel really, really disgusted with my mother.
Under Eye:	I feel really bitter about some of the things my mother has done and not done.
Under Nose:	I absolutely resent some of the things my mother has said and not said.
Chin:	I feel really, really exhausted by my mother.
Collarbone:	I feel angry, bitter, resentful, and damaged by my mother.
Underarm:	I feel that she does not deserve my forgiveness.
Liver:	Even if she does deserve to be forgiven, it need not come from me.
Wrists:	I understand that I'm carrying around a mountain of unforgiveness.
Crown of Head:	I am so profoundly angry with her that I have no other choice.

ROUND 2

Tap 7 times on each meridian point while repeating out loud either the statements below or your reminder phrases.

Eyebrow:	I keep beating my mother up about the past.
Side of Eye:	I'm not going to let her get away with the damage she's done to me.
Under Eye:	What if forgiving my mother could eliminate the pain and hurt from my life?
Under Nose:	What if I just open my heart to releasing a little bit of this rage?
Chin:	What if I acknowledge that my mother did the best she could?
Collarbone:	I don't believe that. She did not do the best she could in my life.
Underarm:	What if I just choose to forgive my mother, just as I would forgive anyone else?
Liver:	What if what she did was the best she knew how to do at the time?
Wrists:	What if forgiving my mother, showing her some compassion, takes me into a state of peace and freedom, joy, and happiness?
Crown of Head:	What if I forgive her and nothing happens? Nothing changes?

ROUND 3

Tap **7** times on each meridian point while repeating out loud either the statements below or your reminder phrases.

Eyebrow:	Forgiving my mother doesn't mean I am not entitled to my feelings.
Side of Eye:	What if forgiving my mother opens my heart to more love, more joy, more of everything I want?
Under Eye:	What if forgiving my mother is the path to what I really want?
Under Nose:	What if forgiving my mother also means forgiving myself?
Chin:	It's a setup. I'm not going to forgive her.
Collarbone:	Well, I am willing to forgive myself, and perhaps I will forgive her.
Underarm:	In fact, just thinking about feeling better makes forgiving her worth it.
Liver:	Perhaps I can find some other reason to forgive her.
Wrists:	I am at least willing to consider forgiving my mother.
Crown of Head:	Better than that, I am choosing to forgive my mother if it is a good choice I can make for myself.

Have a few sips of water. Take a deep breath in through your nose. Release the breath slowly and softly through your mouth, making the sound "Ahhhhh" as you do so.

RECHECK THE INTENSITY LEVEL

Recheck your intensity level on holding unforgiveness about your mother. If the level is at 8 or higher, repeat the entire 3-Round Tapping Sequence outlined in the bonus Tapping Script (or your self-created script.)

If the level is less than 8, tap on one of the following Modified Set-Up Statements, then perform the 10-point Tapping Sequence on the Forgiveness Statements from your daily journal work.

MODIFIED SET-UP STATEMENT

Use the Modified Set-Up Statement below (or use one that you've written yourself) and repeat it three times while tapping continuously on the Karate Chop point.

- Even though I still have some stubborn judgments about myself and some resistance to letting them go, I am willing to let them go, and I love and accept myself totally and unconditionally.

After you complete the Tapping Sequence on your Forgiveness Statements, recheck your intensity level on holding unforgiveness about your mother.

Depending on your level, continue to repeat the sequence described above until you are at a 0 level of intensity.

_____

_____

_____

_____

_____

_____

_____

_____

_____

_____

_____

_____

Never forget the three powerful resources you always
have available to you: love, prayer, and forgiveness.

—H. JACKSON BROWN, JR.

I Forgive My Father

Holding grievances is an attack on God's plan.

I forgive myself. I forgive my mind.
Only by forgiving my false ideas and beliefs
about others and myself can my mind recognize
the truth that I am still in Love's presence,
safe, healed, and whole.

—Prayer for *A Course in Miracles* Workbook
Lesson 72

– Forgiveness Friend Story by Rev. Candas Ifama Barnes –

For some reason that still is not clear to me, as a very young girl I was terrified in my father's presence. As a black man, born in the midst of the depression in 1920 in the segregated South, my father was a study in contradictions. His opinions seemed to keep him boxed in and limited, yet he had a broad view of the world. He read *The Washington Post* daily and quoted Aristotle. He had a strong affinity for family. He walked to my aunt's, his older sister's house, every day to visit and make sure she had what she needed. He had very particular opinions about how things should be and how people should behave. When things did not go the way he insisted, we paid the price for it. When I did not meet his standards or follow his advice, he just wouldn't speak to me. It could go on for days.

My father did not know his father. He always regretted that his father left his life when he was very young. No one ever taught him who a father is and what a father does. He came from an era when a man was expected to provide. He did that well. We always had plenty of food, adequate clothing, and a lovely home. Yet at the same time he was frugal, almost stingy, not only with money but with his heart. Still, whenever I needed a hand, he always lent it. He just didn't have a clue about how to share his affection. In fact, I remember telling my mother when I was very young that I did not like him.

MY FATHER DID NOT KNOW HIS FATHER.

By the time I started school, everything changed. My father would walk me to the public library. It just made me happy to be with him and get my books. For a long time I could check out only a limited number of books because I had a children's library card. When I turned 10, my father made sure that I got an adult library card, which meant that I could check out as many books as I wanted, and he always helped me carry my books home. Sometimes we would stop along the way to get Butter Brickle ice cream. Those days, those walks were pure heaven for me because I had become daddy's little girl.

I must have been in the third or fourth grade when I had to learn the multiplication tables. My father drilled me daily, and I began to hate him for it. However, before the school year was over, I knew every multiplication table from 1 to 12 because of his relentless drilling.

When I was 15, my mom became very ill. At times, my father was not nice to her during her illness. I remember how he yelled and fussed at her for what seemed to me to be no reason. I saw my mother cry only twice in my life, and one of those times was after my father's fussing at her. One day when she was in the hospital I called her room because I needed some information from her. She did not answer the telephone. When I got home from school that evening, I asked my father if he had spoken to her. As if he were reporting the weather to a room filled with strangers, he told me that she had been moved to the intensive care unit because she had had a heart attack. I discovered later that he'd know her condition since early that morning but had not told me. I also found out that he knew

> I CAME TO REALIZE
> AND ACCEPT
> THAT MY FATHER
> REALLY HAD DONE
> THE BEST HE COULD
> WITH WHAT HE HAD.

my mother was dying of cancer and never said a word.

That evening after dinner my father drove me to the hospital to visit my mom. When I got out of the car to go upstairs, he stayed in the car with my niece, who was too young to visit. When I got to my mother's room, she was in the midst of a crisis. The medical personnel were trying to revive her. I stood there for a while feeling dazed, alone, and totally helpless. I ran back to the car to report to my father that I did not see my mother because of what was happening. He said nothing. We drove home in silence. Shortly after we arrived home the hospital called. My father told me, "Your mom died." Then he put on his coat and hat and left the house. I was home alone. It was Halloween. I was furious with my mother for dying but even more pissed that I was stuck with my father, who was not able to share his heart with me.

After my mother's death, I lived out of a suitcase for the next year and a half, shuttling back and forth between my childhood home and my aunt's home. My father was a minister. He had been assigned to a church in Philadelphia, which kept him away from home for long four-to-five-day weekends. While he was away I stayed with my aunt. When he returned, he insisted I come back to his house. He refused to give me permission to have a stable home with my aunt. I think he felt it wouldn't look right. It would be like shirking his duties as my only living parent. With my mother gone it became very clear that my father would not or could not be there for me.

He had not protected me from being molested when I was younger. And he was not there for me during this crucial time after my mother's death. I never again felt as if I was a priority in his life. I felt like an accessory, an element in his picture-perfect family. When my father was assigned to churches out of town, he simply was not there. In his absence I felt painfully alone. When he was there, I felt like a burden.

In the years after my father had a stroke, I harbored a great deal of anger and resentment about who he was and was not, about what he did and did not do for me. I was in total self-righteous judgment of him. This was fueled by a very intense belief that he should have been different than he was. In the weeks before he passed away, I came to realize and accept that my father really had done the best he could with what he had. I became grateful that even though he often forgot my birthday in the later years, he had given me life, and that was a more precious gift.

I also recognized that my father gave me what was required for me to be a good person and a strong woman. He taught me ethics, respect, morals, values, a desire for lifelong learning, and a thirst for knowing the word of God. I credit my father for teaching me to have a deep love of books and reading. As minister, I have now taken up his mantle. I want people to know the God my father loved. And I choose to be grateful for all of the contradictions.

DAILY FORGIVENESS PROCESS REMINDERS

*For a more detailed explanation
of the Daily Forgiveness Process Guidelines, see pages 45–46.*

1. Find a quiet place where you will not be disturbed for at least 30 to 60 minutes.

2. Still your mind for at least 5 minutes or listen to the *Stillness Meditation*.

3. Listen to the *Forgiveness Prayer* on the accompanying audio program. Then read the Forgiveness Prayer, once silently and once aloud.

4. Scan the Emotional Trigger List on pages 9–14.

5. Write out the 12 Forgiveness Statements for each day's topic on thinking, judging, and believing in your Forgiveness Journal (Days 1–18). Write your Forgiveness Letters (Days 19–21).

6. Perform your Pro EFT™ Forgiveness Tapping Sequences.

7. Process thoughts and feelings consciously through your Forgiveness Journal Reflections.

8. Listen to the *Gratitude Meditation*.

9. Complete the day's practice in quiet reflection or with meditative music.

10. Be sure to do something good for yourself today!

I Forgive Myself for Judging My Father

Today's Forgiveness Practice is about forgiveness of your earthly father. Whether you knew him or not, had a relationship with him or not, your father is one of the reasons you are alive. While many of us may have hurts, wounds, and sorrows attached to our father's presence or absence, forgiveness is the most powerful way to lessen the damages we believe our fathers have caused.

Very often, when a father is absent, emotionally unavailable, or physically or mentally unstable, his impact leaves us asking the unanswerable questions: *Why did he . . . ? Why didn't he . . . ? Why me?* While forgiveness may not answer the inquiries in your heart or mind, compassionate forgiveness of your father can and will eliminate the need to know.

As with all heartfelt, committed forgiveness work, the mind becomes clear and the heart opens to a much deeper understanding of how we are loved by the heavenly Father, whether or not our earthly father was who we needed or wanted him to be. I encourage you to undertake today's practice with a deep compassion for yourself and conscious gratitude for your biological father.

A Prayer of Forgiveness

Blessed Heavenly Father:

Today, I ask for and open myself to receive Your forgiveness for all of the judgments, bitterness, and resentments I have held about and against my earthly father. I ask to be freed from any and all heart sorrow, regret, grief, depression, sadness, or suffering that I have attached to my father and his life. I asked to be lifted above any and all hurts, disappointments and abandonments, anger or rage, and shame or blame that I have associated with my father and his life. I ask that you remind me to remember that, like me, my earthly father is a child of God, welcomed and accepted into Your love. I ask that You remind me to remember that when he wasn't there, You were. What he could not and did not do, You did. I ask that You create in me a clear mind and a loving heart for my father and teach me how to see him from a higher place. I am so grateful to know that I have always been guided, protected, and loved by the Father. I pray for my earthly father to recognize that this is also true for him.

I rest in Thee.

I let it be!

And so it is!

THE FORGIVENESS

DAY 5
JOURNAL WORK

---

*I Forgive
My Father*

– I Forgive My Mind for Thinking –

EXAMPLE

I forgive my mind for thinking my father was an abusive womanizer.

I forgive my mind for thinking my father was
_____

_____

I forgive my mind for thinking my father was not
_____

_____

I forgive my mind for thinking my father should have
_____

_____

I forgive my mind for thinking my father should not have
_____

_____

– I Forgive Myself for Judging –

EXAMPLE

I forgive myself for judging my father for being an alcoholic.

I forgive myself for judging my father for _____

_____

I forgive myself for judging my father for not _____

_____

I forgive myself for judging my father about _____

_____

I forgive myself for judging my father about not _____

_____

– I Forgive Myself for Believing –

EXAMPLE

I forgive myself for believing my father should have made me feel important.

I forgive myself for believing my father made me feel

_____

_____

I forgive myself for believing my father did not make me feel

_____

_____

I forgive myself for believing my father should have made me feel

_____

_____

I forgive myself for believing my father should not have made me feel

_____

_____

– TAPPING SEQUENCE –

Review Basic Tapping Sequence Guidelines on pages 53–59.

1. Review each of the day's 12 Forgiveness Statements out loud. This will help you identify the specific aspects of the issue that you want to tap on.

2. Rate the intensity level of any unforgiveness you hold about today's topic on a scale of 1 to 10. Write the number down.

3. Neutralize all subconscious resistance. Repeat a Reversal Statement 3 times while tapping continuously on the Karate Chop point.

4. Focus on the issue you'll be tapping on. Repeat a Set-Up Statement 3 times while tapping continuously on the Karate Chop point.

5. Tap 7 times on each of the 10 meridian points while repeating out loud the key details from the 12 Forgiveness Statements. This process can be modeled on the bonus Tapping Scripts.

6. Recheck the intensity level of any unforgiveness you hold about today's topic. Write the number down. If the level is at 8 or higher, repeat the entire sequence. If the level is less than 8, tap on a Modified Set-Up Statement, then perform the 10-point Tapping Sequence on your 12 Forgiveness Statements until you are at a 0 level of intensity.

– REFLECTIONS –

_____

_____

_____

_____

_____

_____

_____

_____

_____

_____

_____

_____

_____

_____

Sometimes a person needs to hear you forgive them
so they can start to forgive themselves.

—RACHEL GIBSON, *ANY MAN OF MINE*

I Forgive God

*God's Voice speaks to me
all through the day.*

In constant communication with God,
my mind is listening to the Voice of God
that is calm, always at rest, and wholly certain.
Either God is the Mind with which I think,
or ego is the mind with which I think.

—PRAYER FOR *A COURSE IN MIRACLES* WORKBOOK
LESSON 49

— Forgiveness Story by Iyanla Vanzant —

It is always so much easier to blame someone else rather than accepting responsibility for your experiences. Whether it is a breakdown in a relationship or a lack of financial substance or a failure to fulfill a dream or goal, there must be "someone" to blame. In the realm of human experiences that includes education, socialization, and religious indoctrination, there are few instances where we are taught that each individual has the inherent power and responsibility to create the life he or she desires.

We create with our thoughts, beliefs, and expectations. We create by repeating the behavior patterns that feel comfortable and familiar, whether or not they are productive. We create by conscious choice—focused activity that moves us toward exactly what we want. Or we create experiences with unconscious choice—activity without focus or intent. And we create our lives by default, accepting whatever shows up and attempting to make it what we want it to be.

> WE CREATE WITH OUR THOUGHTS, BELIEFS, AND EXPECTATIONS. WE CREATE BY REPEATING THE BEHAVIOR PATTERNS THAT FEEL COMFORTABLE AND FAMILIAR, WHETHER OR NOT THEY ARE PRODUCTIVE.

Whether or not we know what we are creating or how we are creating it, when things do not turn out the way we desire, our human instincts drive us to look for someone to blame.

For those who recognize and accept that there is a Higher Mind, a Divine Essence, a Spiritual Presence to life, we look to that energy to support, assist, and provide us with the things we need, want, and desire. Some call this presence God. Others call it Spirit. When we get what we want, when our lives reflect the good we desire, we are grateful and trust what we call the Spiritual Presence. When, on the other hand, we are confronted with difficulty or disappointment, we doubt and blame the Spiritual Presence.

MORE OF US THAN WOULD EVER ADMIT ARE ABSOLUTELY *PISSED OFF* WITH GOD FOR THE WAY THINGS SHOW UP OR DON'T SHOW UP IN OUR LIVES.

More of us than would ever admit are absolutely *pissed off* with God for the way things show up or don't show up in our lives. While it may seem irrational and illogical to *blame God* for our choosing the wrong partner, accepting an unfulfilling job, or spending more money than we earn, many of us do just that. We blame God. We hold God responsible for our mother's meanness, for our daddy's absence, for the supervisor's failure to promote us, for Boo-Boo's cheating, and for the fact that we just can't seem to get our lives together. If and when things get really bad, we can call to mind the laundry list of things God didn't do, should have done, needs to do, or will never do for a variety of reasons. Many of us are not even consciously aware that we are angry with God. In fact, we believe that such anger is so unthinkable, we won't even entertain it as a possibility. As a result, we cannot heal it. Without acknowledgment, there can be no healing.

Whether you consider yourself religious, spiritual, somewhere in between, or nowhere on the continuum, your relationship with your Source, Creator, or Divine Essence impacts and affects every relationship in your life, including the relationship you have with yourself.

God is love. God is truth. God is power. Whether you call it God or Life or Spirit, the depth of your connection, reliance, trust, and alignment with something greater than yourself is the primary determinant of how you see and hold yourself, within yourself.

If you think you don't judge God, you have the wrong idea. If you have a judgment about anyone or anything, you have a judgment about God. *You cannot judge the creation without judging the Creator.* Who else would you hold responsible for saving you from a crazed mother, an alcoholic father, a deranged ex-husband, or the IRS. You may not call it God, but when your life goes awry, when a tornado destroys a town, when a child suffers or dies, when your marriage falls to pieces, when you cannot pay your rent, to whom do you look? And what angry judgments come forth?

As you move through today's practice, it is absolutely essential that you give yourself permission to be radically honest and acknowledge any anger, disappointment, and judgments—anything else you are holding about or against God. You may be surprised that once you do this, you'll feel a lot better about yourself.

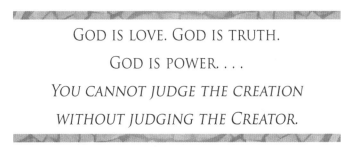

GOD IS LOVE. GOD IS TRUTH.
GOD IS POWER. . . .
YOU CANNOT JUDGE THE CREATION
WITHOUT JUDGING THE CREATOR.

DAILY FORGIVENESS PROCESS REMINDERS

For a more detailed explanation
of the Daily Forgiveness Process Guidelines, see pages 45–46.

1. Find a quiet place where you will not be disturbed for at least 30 to 60 minutes.

2. Still your mind for at least 5 minutes or listen to the *Stillness Meditation*.

3. Listen to the *Forgiveness Prayer* on the accompanying audio program. Then read the Forgiveness Prayer, once silently and once aloud.

4. Scan the Emotional Trigger List on pages 9–14.

5. Write out the 12 Forgiveness Statements for each day's topic on thinking, judging, and believing in your Forgiveness Journal (Days 1–18). Write your Forgiveness Letters (Days 19–21).

6. Perform your Pro EFT™ Forgiveness Tapping Sequences.

7. Process thoughts and feelings consciously through your Forgiveness Journal Reflections.

8. Listen to the *Gratitude Meditation*.

9. Complete the day's practice in quiet reflection or with meditative music.

10. Be sure to do something good for yourself today!

I Forgive Myself for Judging God

Today's Forgiveness Practice is about forgiving the judgments, anger, disappointments, hurts, and wounds that may be buried in your consciousness and are directed toward God. Although the thought of it may be frightening, if you are human, chances are there is something for which you are holding your Creator totally responsible and accountable. Start by considering all the experiences you may have judged as wrong, unfair, unkind, or unloving, whether you were directly involved or not.

GOD ALREADY
KNOWS . . .

As always, today's practice is designed to neutralize what is going on within you in order to make space for new and greater possibilities to unfold. If there is a part of you, be it large or small, that is terrified of the possibility of acknowledging this to yourself and to God, just consider this: *What exactly is it that you think God doesn't know about you?* It is quite possible that because God already knows it, the deeper healing will come when you are ready to admit it to yourself.

A Prayer of Forgiveness

Precious Lord of the Universe of Life:

Today, I ask for and open myself to receive an outpouring of Your mercy and grace. I ask that You open my mind so that I will know the truth. I ask that You open my heart so that I will experience the truth. I ask that You open my eyes so that I will see all of the places within myself and within my life where I have been in doubt, denial, resistance, and avoidance of Your presence.

Because I know that You do not judge me, I ask You to allow me to feel, see, hear, think about, and know how I have dismissed, diminished, and judged You. Allow me to know and feel my connection to You. Help me to recognize my projections and to look within myself for all that I have cast onto You.

Move me beyond any and all shame or blame at their deepest root and cause so that I will know the joy of being in intimate union with You. Teach me how to forgive You. Remind me that in Your love my safety and freedom reside.

I rest in Thee.

I let it be!

And so it is!

THE FORGIVENESS

DAY 6
JOURNAL WORK

I Forgive God

– I Forgive My Mind for Thinking –

EXAMPLE

I forgive my mind for thinking that God does not really exist.

I forgive my mind for thinking God is

_____

_____

I forgive my mind for thinking God is not

_____

_____

I forgive my mind for thinking God did

_____

_____

I forgive my mind for thinking God did not

_____

_____

– I FORGIVE MYSELF FOR JUDGING –

EXAMPLE

I forgive myself for judging God as weak and mean and unloving for all the horrible things that have happened to me and to the world.

I forgive myself for judging God for _____

_____

I forgive myself for judging God for not _____

_____

I forgive myself for judging God as responsible for _____

_____

I forgive myself for judging God as irresponsible for _____

_____

– I Forgive Myself for Believing –

EXAMPLE

I forgive myself for believing that God was powerless, cruel, and responsible for all the bad things that have happened to me.

I forgive myself for believing God should

_____

_____

I forgive myself for believing God should not

_____

_____

I forgive myself for believing God has

_____

_____

I forgive myself for believing God has never

_____

_____

– TAPPING SEQUENCE –

Review Basic Tapping Sequence Guidelines on pages 53–59.

1. Review each of the day's 12 Forgiveness Statements out loud. This will help you identify the specific aspects of the issue that you want to tap on.

2. Rate the intensity level of any unforgiveness you hold about today's topic on a scale of 1 to 10. Write the number down.

3. Neutralize all subconscious resistance. Repeat a Reversal Statement 3 times while tapping continuously on the Karate Chop point.

4. Focus on the issue you'll be tapping on. Repeat a Set-Up Statement 3 times while tapping continuously on the Karate Chop point.

5. Tap 7 times on each of the 10 meridian points while repeating out loud the key details from the 12 Forgiveness Statements. This process can be modeled on the bonus Tapping Scripts.

6. Recheck the intensity level of any unforgiveness you hold about today's topic. Write the number down. If the level is at 8 or higher, repeat the entire sequence. If the level is less than 8, tap on a Modified Set-Up Statement, then perform the 10-point Tapping Sequence on your 12 Forgiveness Statements until you are at a 0 level of intensity.

– REFLECTIONS –

_____

_____

_____

_____

_____

_____

_____

_____

_____

_____

_____

_____

As I walked out the door toward the gate that would
lead to my freedom, I knew if I didn't leave my bitterness and hatred behind, I'd still be in prison.

—NELSON MANDELA

I Forgive
My Feelings

*I am upset because I see something
that is not there.*

If my emotions indicate to me that I am upset,
not feeling the peace of God, it is only ever because
I see something that is not there, something that is
an image and representation of a thought.
Any upset feeling is an indicator that I am
ready to forgive.

—PRAYER FOR *A COURSE IN MIRACLES WORKBOOK*
LESSON 6

— Forgiveness Story by Iyanla Vanzant —

I didn't like her. At the time, I was not sure why, nor did I care to know why—all I knew was that she made my skin crawl. Perhaps she was just too sweet, always going out of her way to do something nice for someone. Or maybe it was the way she always attempted to see the good in other people, especially the ones I held in total disdain.

Did that stop her from treating me with kindness and respect? No! I did everything in my power to let her know that she was not my cup of tea. Did that stop her from bringing me gifts? No! Where my short, curt, often sarcastic responses to her endless questions about the state of my health and well-being a deterrent? No! Her mere presence got on my nerves! She rubbed me the wrong way!

> WHY WOULD ANYONE BE NICE TO ME?

I hated her hair, the way she dressed, her high-pitched laughter, and how her scent lingered in a room long after she left it. My mother-in-law was a royal pain in my butt, and I felt ashamed, embarrassed, and sad about the way I felt about her. I wanted to like her. I just couldn't do it because she represented pieces and parts of myself that I had failed to recognize, understand, or embrace.

I grew up in a family where very few people were nice to me. The story I told myself was that the big people in my life tolerated my presence until they needed me to do something for them. Then and only then would they say something nice to me or smile at me. The children in my family took their cues from the big people. I was the butt of most of the jokes, and I got blamed for almost everything. As a result, I developed a healthy suspicion of most people, particularly nice people. *Why would anyone be nice to me?* If my father, brother, sister, other relatives, and houseguests treated me with disdain, anyone who was being nice to me must want something—or must be crazy. In any event, whatever they wanted, even if it was a simple answer to a harmless, benign question, I was not going to give it to them.

One day at work, a person I rarely interacted with said something to me that sat me down in shock.

"You are such a nice person. You are always willing to help other people, and that is a very admirable quality."

"Who, me?"

"Yes, you. I think people misunderstand you because you don't say much, and when you do, it can sound rather harsh. But I see how you never go to lunch without asking if you can bring back something. I see how you always pick up copies from the machine and distribute them. I see how you always fill the candy jar on your desk and never complain when it's all gone by the end of the day. Those are nice things you do, and I notice them. Thank you."

I thought she had lost her mind. The truth is, without a moment's reflection, I lost mine. When I heard her words, I lost the hard, suspicious, wounded, broken parts of my mind that prevented me from seeing the truth about myself. I lost years of childhood memories and slights and wounds that had allowed me to see only what I thought was the worst of me in everyone else. I lost all of the anger that I could not express toward the big people in my childhood homes. More important, I lost my suspicion of nice people. If I was one of them, I certainly could not be mean and nasty toward them. That would mean I had to be mean to myself. That was something I couldn't knowingly do because there were enough other people in my life who had had that job.

The day after my daughter was born, my mother-in-law said something that would change our relationship and my life.

"You remind me so much of myself when I was younger. I was so angry and very arrogant. I was angry because I was hurt. I was arrogant because everyone I knew and loved had failed to acknowledge how deeply they had hurt me. I spent the better part of my life mad at the world until I learned to forgive. I hope that now that you are a mother you will learn how to forgive, because you are going to need that saving grace one day. Children have a funny way of breaking your heart—many times over."

With that, she kissed my daughter, then me, and left the room.

If only someone had told me that I had a right to be angry at my mother for dying and leaving me, it would have saved me years of grief. Had I known when I was sitting on the steps waiting for my father, knowing he was not going to show up, that I had permission to hit something or say something, it would have helped me understand what I was feeling. As children we are often told what not to feel and what not to say. As a result, we often grow into adults who believe that what we feel is wrong and what we want to say is not nice. The result is that we judge what we feel, believing it is unacceptable. When what we feel in our hearts is unacceptable, we can become emotionally dishonest and/or disconnected. When we disconnect from our hearts, our feelings, our emotional being, we also disconnect from our personal power. True power comes from the heart, not the head.

> TRUE POWER COMES FROM THE HEART, NOT THE HEAD.

Feelings come and they pass. Whatever we are feeling in any given moment is just a passing experience. Our work is to learn to accept what we feel and to learn to let it pass. If not, we can get stuck in judging our instinctive responses to people and circumstances. When that happens, forgiveness is the only ticket out and up.

DAILY FORGIVENESS PROCESS REMINDERS

*For a more detailed explanation
of the Daily Forgiveness Process Guidelines, see pages 45–46.*

1. Find a quiet place where you will not be disturbed for at least 30 to 60 minutes.

2. Still your mind for at least 5 minutes or listen to the *Stillness Meditation.*

3. Listen to the *Forgiveness Prayer* on the accompanying audio program. Then read the Forgiveness Prayer, once silently and once aloud.

4. Scan the Emotional Trigger List on pages 9–14.

5. Write out the 12 Forgiveness Statements for each day's topic on thinking, judging, and believing in your Forgiveness Journal (Days 1–18). Write your Forgiveness Letters (Days 19–21).

6. Perform your Pro EFT™ Forgiveness Tapping Sequences.

7. Process thoughts and feelings consciously through your Forgiveness Journal Reflections.

8. Listen to the *Gratitude Meditation.*

9. Complete the day's practice in quiet reflection or with meditative music.

10. Be sure to do something good for yourself today!

I Forgive Myself for Judging My Feelings

Today's Forgiveness Practice is about forgiving your feelings or emotional responses. Have you ever felt crappy, treated other people in a crappy way, and then beat yourself up for it? Well, if you have, it means you're truly human, and that's not fatal. Emotions or feelings are the energy that moves us. They are influenced by our internal landscape, the environment, stress, our diet, even newspaper headlines! In other words, what we feel in any given moment is a function of many factors, some of which we may not be aware of.

For today's practice, give yourself permission to really examine the places where you believe you should not feel what you feel. Be mindful not to label anything as good or bad, right or wrong. Reflect and review on the situations, circumstances, and relationships where emotional dishonesty, shutdown, or disconnection may be at play, and forgive whatever you feel.

> EMOTIONS OR FEELINGS ARE THE ENERGY THAT MOVES US.

A Prayer of Forgiveness

Dear God:

Thank you for making the entire human race and me so wonderfully complex. You have given us free will. You have blessed us with the powers of thought and choice. You have filled us with the capacity to love, and You know the depths to which we fall when love is not present. Today, I ask for and open myself to receive a total and complete healing of any and all toxic emotions at their deepest roots and causes. I give You complete and total permission to allow You to lift any unproductive, un-loving energy that can be lifted and to transform them into pure white light. I ask that You create in me a clean heart and restore me to a state of innocence and grace. For this and so much more, I am so grateful.

I let it be as You desire!

And so it is!

THE FORGIVENESS

DAY 7
JOURNAL WORK

---

*I Forgive
My Feelings*

– I Forgive My Mind for Thinking –

EXAMPLE

I forgive my mind for thinking I shouldn't be feeling disappointed about not being further along in my life than I am now.

I forgive my mind for thinking I should feel

_____

_____

I forgive my mind for thinking I should not feel

_____

_____

I forgive my mind for thinking my feelings are

_____

_____

I forgive my mind for thinking my feelings are not

_____

_____

– I Forgive Myself for Judging –

EXAMPLE

I forgive myself for judging what I feel as unimportant.

I forgive myself for judging what I feel as

_____

_____

I forgive myself for judging what I don't feel as

_____

_____

I forgive myself for judging my feelings as

_____

_____

I forgive myself for not judging my feelings as

_____

_____

– I Forgive Myself for Believing –

EXAMPLE

I forgive myself for believing my feelings won't be heard.

I forgive myself for believing my feelings are _____

_____

I forgive myself for believing my feelings are not _____

_____

I forgive myself for believing my feelings always _____

_____

I forgive myself for believing my feelings never _____

_____

– TAPPING SEQUENCE –

Review Basic Tapping Sequence Guidelines on pages 53–59.

1. Review each of the day's 12 Forgiveness Statements out loud. This will help you identify the specific aspects of the issue that you want to tap on.

2. Rate the intensity level of any unforgiveness you hold about today's topic on a scale of 1 to 10. Write the number down.

3. Neutralize all subconscious resistance. Repeat a Reversal Statement 3 times while tapping continuously on the Karate Chop point.

4. Focus on the issue you'll be tapping on. Repeat a Set-Up Statement 3 times while tapping continuously on the Karate Chop point.

5. Tap 7 times on each of the 10 meridian points while repeating out loud the key details from the 12 Forgiveness Statements. This process can be modeled on the bonus Tapping Scripts.

6. Recheck the intensity level of any unforgiveness you hold about today's topic. Write the number down. If the level is at 8 or higher, repeat the entire sequence. If the level is less than 8, tap on a Modified Set-Up Statement, then perform the 10-point Tapping Sequence on your 12 Forgiveness Statements until you are at a 0 level of intensity.

_____
_____
_____
_____
_____
_____
_____
_____
_____
_____
_____
_____
_____

Forgiveness is not always easy. At times, it feels more painful
than the wound we suffered, to forgive the one who
inflicted it. And yet, there is no peace without forgiveness.

—MARIANNE WILLIAMSON

I Forgive My Weaknesses and Failures

God has condemned me not. No more do I.

God does not condemn me with His Thoughts
about me. Why then would I deny His Thoughts
and choose thoughts that condemn me?
With my own choice of thoughts I make my reality,
my self-perception, my perception of everything
that seems to happen to me.
I choose everything that I see.

—Prayer for *A Course in Miracles Workbook*
Lesson 228

– Forgiveness Friend Story by Rev. Lydia Ruiz –

In August 1993, his story was reported in the *New York Daily News*. After watching an HBO movie titled *Strapped,* a 15-year-old boy decided to reenact the story in his own life. He went out to Greenwich Village in New York City. He returned home with a heart filled with anxiety. He was unable to pull the trigger. Plan B: he decided to shoot out a window toward a basketball park filled with players. My mother had just returned home after completing a nine-day rosary vigil for a neighbor who had lost her mother. My mother was preparing her dinner when he pulled the trigger.

The first time I saw him, it was in Judge Judy's courtroom. She was a courtroom judge before she became a television icon. In classic Judge Judy style she asked, "Well, what do you have to say for yourself, young man?" He stood stark still, glaring ahead of himself as if he were watching television. He had nothing to say. According to the defense attorney, his mother was an active alcoholic who was not in the courtroom. My mother was dead. Yet for some reason I was sitting in court feeling sorrow and sadness for the child who had senselessly murdered her. She was the bedrock of my foundation. I hated him for what he had done—stupid kid!

My mother's death made me an orphan at age 37. I grew up in hardcore streets of New York City, Spanish Harlem, where the street rules were, "Don't cuss in front of my mother!" and "You better not talk about my mother" and "I will kill you if you touch my mother!" This was all well and good when I was talking to my peers, but a kid???? How was I supposed to retaliate? How would I avenge her death?

My family, friends, and the neighborhood who knew my mother as the "praying hairdresser" were all outraged, looking at me, wondering—like I was—what I was going to do. There were marches and protests to influence his sentencing. The local politicians she had worked with used her death as a springboard to advance their careers. It was an opportunity to extract justice for a senseless murder and a forgotten community. But I couldn't sleep at night. My eyes were so swollen from crying, I could barely see. No matter where we were or what was going on, every now and again my sister would let out these bloodcurdling screams in an effort to release her pain. It was unbearable. The possibilities were unspeakable.

I wanted revenge. I wanted justice. I wanted to hurt someone, anyone—as if that would make my pain easier to bear. One night I met with an old associate who I knew had a gun. He said he knew I would come. I wondered why he thought this was what people were waiting for and what was expected. It felt like my legs had a mind of their own. I went to the one place I knew my mother would want me to be—the church. It was her second home. She cleaned it, decorated it, and sat there many a times in the echoic silence. I sat in her pew. I called out her name. Unlike many other times, this time she didn't answer. I called out to God. His response was clear: *"You have been sick for too many years. The freedom your mother prayed for is here. Your addiction is now released. What will you do? What have you learned from the gift of living? How will you go on to get your life in order?"*

Forgiveness immediately came to my mind. But I was too angry and hurt even to consider it. Who needed forgiveness anyway? Was it me, for spending so much time in addiction and away from my mother? Or was it the damaged, dysfunctional child who had taken her life? Forgiveness felt like a plan in the future, not for the justifiable pain of the moment. Forgiveness was what God would do for him. It wasn't my job. I had to wake up without my mother in my childhood home. I had to clean up all the stuff she left behind. I had to look through her things and discover her own soul searching that she had documented in her Bible. I found her handwritten notes, her prayers to God. As I read them I realized how blessed I was to have had a mother who had prayed for me.

Those prayers helped to soften my heart. I thought about her murderer, a child with a television and a gun, who had no guidance or support; a boy who did not have a mother like mine. I remembered how happy my mother had been when I finally got clean. She was so proud of me. I wondered if his mother had ever prayed for him? Or if she had been drunk all of his life? What could I do to preserve her prayers? This time she did answer: *"The same love and prayers you received, the ones that changed your life, are the same prayers you offer for others."* But I wanted him to suffer.

For the next three years I was absolutely miserable. Sleepless nights, exaggerated mood swings, feelings of loss and hopelessness that I could not shake. When I thought about him and my dead mother—and me not doing anything about it—the anger became unbearable. *How can I pray for him? How can I forgive him? Who and what would I become if I continued holding on to unforgiveness?* I felt right in my position but wrong in my soul. I felt disconnected from God, which I knew meant I was disconnected from my mother. It was all ego—*edging God out*—so I could keep my self-righteous feelings. It was the ruthlessness of my ego reigning supreme in my mind.

So what do I know about forgiveness? Forgiveness is a silent, intimate teacher. She is always ready to bring the lessons you need, whether or not you want to learn. Forgiveness is the mother who soothes the rough edges of your life, enabling the willing heart and mind to surrender.

> FORGIVENESS IS A SILENT, INTIMATE TEACHER. SHE IS ALWAYS READY TO BRING THE LESSONS YOU NEED, WHETHER OR NOT YOU WANT TO LEARN.

I had to make a choice. I chose peace. I chose a solid, intimate relationship with God as the path to an eternal relationship with my mother. Forgiveness is the path to peace. It doesn't have to make sense, and you don't have to want to do it. What I wanted was to create a new street code for myself. Through forgiveness God now had a way to speak to me. I still hear it most of the time. It is the voice of love. I now know that forgiveness is the voice of love that turns all weakness into strength.

DAILY FORGIVENESS
PROCESS REMINDERS

*For a more detailed explanation
of the Daily Forgiveness Process Guidelines, see pages 45–46.*

1. Find a quiet place where you will not be disturbed for at least 30 to 60 minutes.

2. Still your mind for at least 5 minutes or listen to the *Stillness Meditation*.

3. Listen to the *Forgiveness Prayer* on the accompanying audio program. Then read the Forgiveness Prayer, once silently and once aloud.

4. Scan the Emotional Trigger List on pages 9–14.

5. Write out the 12 Forgiveness Statements for each day's topic on thinking, judging, and believing in your Forgiveness Journal (Days 1–18). Write your Forgiveness Letters (Days 19–21).

6. Perform your Pro EFT™ Forgiveness Tapping Sequences.

7. Process thoughts and feelings consciously through your Forgiveness Journal Reflections.

8. Listen to the *Gratitude Meditation*.

9. Complete the day's practice in quiet reflection or with meditative music.

10. Be sure to do something good for yourself today!

I Forgive Myself for Judging My Weaknesses and Failures

Today's Forgiveness Practice is about forgiving what we judge as weaknesses within ourselves and the experiences we perceive as failures. Weaknesses and failures can keep you stuck in shame, guilt, and self-doubt. As human beings, we are prone to prize perfection. When we judge ourselves as imperfect, self-criticism will take the place of compassion in our minds and hearts. All things are lessons that God would have us learn. Unfortunately, if we don't know that class is in session, we can judge the things we do and the things that happen to be bad, wrong, and personal failures. With today's practice we will take those judgments to the table of forgiveness. You are encouraged to consider relationships, work experiences, hopes, wishes, dreams, and incomplete cycles of actions—things you began but did not complete. And be sure to forgive the feelings and beliefs about yourself that you have attached to these so-called weaknesses and failures.

> **ALL THINGS ARE LESSONS THAT GOD WOULD HAVE US LEARN.**

A Prayer of Forgiveness

My Dear Lord:

Help me!

Help me to remember what I desire and to forget what I have done.

Help me to forget what I haven't done so that I will remember what I can do.

Help me to hear and know Your voice, when You are guiding me, inspiring me, and leading me into new experiences, new opportunities, and new possibilities.

Help me to see new ways of being as I release old ways of seeing.

Help me to release.

Help me to surrender.

Help me today.

I rest in Thee.

I let it be!

And so it is!

THE FORGIVENESS

DAY 8
JOURNAL WORK

---

*I FORGIVE MY
WEAKNESSES
AND FAILURES*

– I Forgive My Mind for Thinking –

EXAMPLE

I forgive my mind for thinking I am weak when I don't speak up for myself.

I forgive my mind for thinking I am weak because

_____

_____

I forgive my mind for thinking I am weak when

_____

_____

I forgive my mind for thinking I failed at

_____

_____

I forgive my mind for thinking I failed when

_____

_____

– I Forgive Myself for Judging –

EXAMPLE

I forgive myself for judging myself as a failure because I was passed over for a promotion at work.

I forgive myself for judging myself as weak because

_____

_____

I forgive myself for judging myself as a failure because

_____

_____

I forgive myself for judging myself as weak when

_____

_____

I forgive myself for judging myself as a failure when

_____

_____

– I Forgive Myself for Believing –

EXAMPLE

I forgive myself for believing I failed in college and that I'm too old to go back now.

I forgive myself for believing I am weak because

_____

_____

I forgive myself for believing I am weak because

_____

_____

I forgive myself for believing I am weak because

_____

_____

I forgive myself for believing I am weak because

_____

_____

– TAPPING SEQUENCE –

Review Basic Tapping Sequence Guidelines on pages 53–59.

1. Review each of the day's 12 Forgiveness Statements out loud. This will help you identify the specific aspects of the issue that you want to tap on.

2. Rate the intensity level of any unforgiveness you hold about today's topic on a scale of 1 to 10. Write the number down.

3. Neutralize all subconscious resistance. Repeat a Reversal Statement 3 times while tapping continuously on the Karate Chop point.

4. Focus on the issue you'll be tapping on. Repeat a Set-Up Statement 3 times while tapping continuously on the Karate Chop point.

5. Tap 7 times on each of the 10 meridian points while repeating out loud the key details from the 12 Forgiveness Statements. This process can be modeled on the bonus Tapping Scripts.

6. Recheck the intensity level of any unforgiveness you hold about today's topic. Write the number down. If the level is at 8 or higher, repeat the entire sequence. If the level is less than 8, tap on a Modified Set-Up Statement, then perform the 10-point Tapping Sequence on your 12 Forgiveness Statements until you are at a 0 level of intensity.

– REFLECTIONS –

_____
_____
_____

_____
_____
_____
_____
_____

_____
_____
_____
_____

Instead of slapping your forehead and asking, "What was I thinking,"
breathe and ask yourself the kinder question, "What was I learning?"

—KAREN SALMANSOHN

I FORGIVE MY CHOICES

I am affected only by my thoughts.

My thoughts can frighten me, but since they are
my thoughts, I have the power to change and
exchange them. It is in my own best interest
to train my mind to be affected only by the thoughts
I do desire. I deliberately choose
the thoughts I desire. I choose the feelings
I experience. I forgive the conflicting
ideas that harm me.

—PRAYER FOR *A COURSE IN MIRACLES WORKBOOK*
LESSON 338

I love you and I forgive you for everything.

On August 16, 2012, I wrote these words to my mother. For three and a half years, I had been in a process of forgiveness. Sitting on the edge of my bed halfway under the covers with tears streaming down my face, my Holy Instant arrived, and I pressed send. It was 6:20 p.m., and I was filled with a deep sense of peace and contentment. There was no longer any anger, judgment, blame, or pain. The story was no longer important to tell. This time the freedom of forgiveness was all that mattered. I wept because I remembered the time that she had come knocking, a time when I wasn't ready. What a difference a moment can make when we choose to heal.

I thought about the Christmas Day when I asked my mother if she wanted to talk. I had planned it to be our first exchange about a very old hurt and deep wound. I thought that I wanted to hear her version of why she never came back for me. As a bonus, she would get to hear my version of how she broke my heart, shattered my life, and left me with no compass or understanding of life and love. We sat in a small room while the rest of the family exchanged laughter; we exchanged hearts. With each story, we wept. We wept until we could no longer speak. She "just didn't know how to love [me] and had no clue how to be a mother." In that moment, I saw her innocence as my own. In that moment, my heart opened to her love and the possibility of forgiveness. In that moment, however, it was still just a possibility.

From speaking with my mother I learned that forgiveness is a process that begins with the choice to end your own suffering. It is also a moment-by-moment choice. It is also a simple choice—suffering or joy, bondage or freedom. I have chosen to see things differently. Regardless of how I judged what she could have or should have done better, she did the only thing she knew how to do at the moment. The biggest choice for me was surrendering the need to understand. I will never understand. There are some things no one can ever understand.

Today, I no longer view my mother through a lens of pain, nor do I see the choices she made as the source of my pain. I choose to see her as a woman, and just like me, there were days when she felt unworthy and unlovable.

> WHAT A DIFFERENCE
> A MOMENT CAN
> MAKE WHEN WE
> CHOOSE TO HEAL.

Just like me, she made choices that she is not proud of making. Just like me, she has suffered from feelings of guilt, shame, and anger. I guess she has had her share of heartbreak and wants to experience the forgiving power of the love. And just like me, she wants to know that she is forgiven. I choose to let her know that, in my soul, all is well.

DAILY FORGIVENESS
PROCESS REMINDERS

*For a more detailed explanation
of the Daily Forgiveness Process Guidelines, see pages 45–46.*

1. Find a quiet place where you will not be disturbed for at least 30 to 60 minutes.

2. Still your mind for at least 5 minutes or listen to the *Stillness Meditation.*

3. Listen to the *Forgiveness Prayer* on the accompanying audio program. Then read the Forgiveness Prayer, once silently and once aloud.

4. Scan the Emotional Trigger List on pages 9–14.

5. Write out the 12 Forgiveness Statements for each day's topic on thinking, judging, and believing in your Forgiveness Journal (Days 1–18). Write your Forgiveness Letters (Days 19–21).

6. Perform your Pro EFT™ Forgiveness Tapping Sequences.

7. Process thoughts and feelings consciously through your Forgiveness Journal Reflections.

8. Listen to the *Gratitude Meditation.*

9. Complete the day's practice in quiet reflection or with meditative music.

10. Be sure to do something good for yourself today!

I FORGIVE MYSELF FOR JUDGING MY CHOICES

Today's Forgiveness Practice is about judging past choices. A choice is a focused intention that provides the creative catalyst and energetic call to all action. Without choice, there can be no movement. With choice, mental programming is rendered void—if only for a moment.

Unfortunately, many of the choices we make moment by moment are fueled by what we believe about the past and what we fear about the future. For this reason, no choice is a bad choice; every choice is an opportunity for learning to unfold. In today's practice you are encouraged to examine and explore those choices you have made, regardless of the results, and those that you have second-guessed. It is also an opportunity to explore the choices you are hesitant about making today.

> NO CHOICE
> IS A BAD CHOICE;
> EVERY CHOICE
> IS AN OPPORTUNITY
> FOR LEARNING
> TO UNFOLD.

A Prayer of Forgiveness

There is nothing to be healed only God to be revealed.

I now ask that the peace of God be revealed in my mind. There is nothing to be healed only God to be revealed. I now ask that the love of God be revealed in my heart. There is nothing to be healed only God to be revealed. I now ask that the will of God be revealed in every choice I make. There is nothing to be healed only God to be revealed. I now ask that the presence of God be revealed in all that I do.

There is nothing to be healed only God to be revealed. I now ask that the perfect peace of God be revealed in my life.

Today, I ask for and open myself to experience the presence of God in my mind, my heart, and every other aspect of my life.

For the blessings of this day I am so grateful.

I rest in Thee.

I let it be!

And so it is!

THE FORGIVENESS

DAY 9
JOURNAL WORK

*I Forgive
My Choices*

– I Forgive My Mind for Thinking –

EXAMPLE

I forgive myself for thinking I should not have left my job when I did.

I forgive my mind for thinking I should have chosen

_____

_____

I forgive my mind for thinking I should not have chosen

_____

_____

I forgive my mind for thinking that I cannot choose

_____

_____

I forgive my mind for thinking I will not choose

_____

_____

– I FORGIVE MYSELF FOR JUDGING –

EXAMPLE

I forgive myself for judging my choice to remain single and never have children.

I forgive myself for judging my choice to

_____

_____

I forgive myself for not judging my choice to

_____

_____

I forgive myself for judging myself when I chose to

_____

_____

I forgive myself for judging myself when I chose not to

_____

_____

– I Forgive Myself for Believing –

EXAMPLE

I forgive myself for choosing to believe that I cannot turn my life in a new direction.

I forgive myself for choosing to believe

_____

_____

I forgive myself for choosing not be believe

_____

_____

I forgive myself for believing that it was wrong for me to choose

_____

_____

I forgive myself for believing that it was wrong for me to choose not to

_____

_____

– TAPPING SEQUENCE –

Review Basic Tapping Sequence Guidelines on pages 53–59.

1. Review each of the day's 12 Forgiveness Statements out loud. This will help you identify the specific aspects of the issue that you want to tap on.

2. Rate the intensity level of any unforgiveness you hold about today's topic on a scale of 1 to 10. Write the number down.

3. Neutralize all subconscious resistance. Repeat a Reversal Statement 3 times while tapping continuously on the Karate Chop point.

4. Focus on the issue you'll be tapping on. Repeat a Set-Up Statement 3 times while tapping continuously on the Karate Chop point.

5. Tap 7 times on each of the 10 meridian points while repeating out loud the key details from the 12 Forgiveness Statements. This process can be modeled on the bonus Tapping Scripts.

6. Recheck the intensity level of any unforgiveness you hold about today's topic. Write the number down. If the level is at 8 or higher, repeat the entire sequence. If the level is less than 8, tap on a Modified Set-Up Statement, then perform the 10-point Tapping Sequence on your 12 Forgiveness Statements until you are at a 0 level of intensity.

_____

_____

_____

_____

_____

_____

_____

_____

_____

_____

_____

_____

Forgiveness is not forgetting; it is simply
denying your pain the right to control your life.

—Corallie Buchanan,
Watch Out! Godly Women on the Loose

I Forgive My Relationship with Money

I have no cause for anger or for fear,
for You surround me. And in every need that
I perceive, Your grace suffices me.

Father, let me remember You are here, surrounding me
with Your everlasting Love, perfect peace, and joy. I pivot
my attention to the natural dwelling place of my mind, my
natural awareness. These are the thoughts that move and
keep my mind safe in You, free of the ego's ideas that
hurt me. Let me remember You are here, and
I am not alone.

—Prayer for *A Course in Miracles Workbook*
Lesson 348

— Forgiveness Story by Iyanla Vanzant —

I grew up in a paycheck-to-paycheck mentality. My mom got paid every other Friday. I loved payday Fridays because it meant we would go to the supermarket to get all of the things we needed to fill the fridge and cupboards. It gave me a sense of security to see two or three bottles of milk and a full loaf of bread. Payday meant that at least for a few days I didn't have to think about eating too much or about there not being enough of the basics for breakfast, lunch, or dinner. Two or three days before payday it was a totally different story. On those days, I knew to make only half of a sandwich and drink only half of a glass of milk in order to stretch what we had until we had more. I carried this pattern in my life as an adult—everything had to be gone before I could have more. This was especially true when it came to my relationship with money.

When I decided to put my grandson in a private high school, I had no idea how I was going to pay for it. At the time, I was barely covering the basics, but I knew that public school was not an option for him. I was able to get a personal-education loan to get him into the school, and I was going to

WHEN YOU HAVE A PAYCHECK-TO-PAYCHECK MENTALITY, IT IS DIFFICULT TO SEE THE POSSIBILITY OF HAVING MORE THAN ENOUGH.

figure out a way to pay the monthly tuition. By the end of his freshman year, I was four months behind; the school notified me that in order for him to return to school, his tuition payments had to be up-to-date. When you have a paycheck-to-paycheck mentality, it is difficult to see the possibility of having more than enough. In my life it seemed that I could never have enough money. This made "more than enough" a mission impossible. It was during this period of my life that I found a book by Catherine Ponder titled *Open Your Mind to Receive*.

> HAVING WHAT YOU NEED AND DESIRE IS NOT A REWARD FOR WHAT YOU DO. INSTEAD, IT IS A FUNCTION OF HOW YOU THINK AND WHAT YOU BELIEVE.

I had never considered money, wealth, prosperity, or abundance to be a function of receiving. What I learned as a child was that you must work hard to get money, and when you do get it, you have to make it last in order to have enough. Catherine Ponder introduced me to a new way of thinking. Having what you need and desire is not a reward for what you do. Instead, it is a function of how you think and what you believe. The universe of life responds to our dominant thoughts. Ponder acknowledged that most people think of money as a thing—a thing you must work hard to get. In the pages of her book I discovered that the positive energy of what we *desire* is far more productive and attractive than the fear-based, often negative energy of what we *need* or want. I also

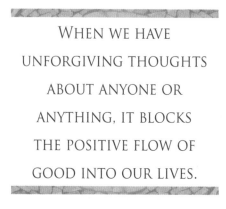

WHEN WE HAVE UNFORGIVING THOUGHTS ABOUT ANYONE OR ANYTHING, IT BLOCKS THE POSITIVE FLOW OF GOOD INTO OUR LIVES.

learned that when we have unforgiving thoughts about anyone or anything, it blocks the positive flow of good into our lives. It was clear. Money is a good thing, and I was preventing it from flowing through my life. The patterns I learned as a child was one level of prevention. All the people I was still angry with were another.

If it meant that my grandson would get a good education, I was willing to consider forgiving some people. If it meant that I could pay all of the bills and still have something left over, I would give anything a try. If forgiving my parents, the man who violated me, the people who had abandoned me, and the people who just didn't like me meant I could go to bed at night, sleep peacefully, and awaken the next morning without the fear that someone was going to show up at my door to take something away or cut something off, I would do anything.

Ponder said to write down what I wanted and to forgive myself for not having it. She said to speak words of forgiveness until I believed them. She said to stop trying to control how the money would come and instead give thanks that what I desired was mine for the asking. It was hard to believe that money could come to me without my doing anything to make that happen—but it did. It was even more difficult for me to adjust my mind to accept that by forgiving the people who had failed to provide me with what I needed and wanted I would receive all that I desired—but I did. By no means was it easy to adjust, change, or live beyond my childhood money patterns and all the myths I had learned about money; however, as Ponder wrote: "There is a healing power to releasing what was that allows you to receive what is and will always be—more than enough."

DAILY FORGIVENESS PROCESS REMINDERS

*For a more detailed explanation
of the Daily Forgiveness Process Guidelines, see pages 45–46.*

1. Find a quiet place where you will not be disturbed for at least 30 to 60 minutes.

2. Still your mind for at least 5 minutes or listen to the *Stillness Meditation*.

3. Listen to the *Forgiveness Prayer* on the accompanying audio program. Then read the Forgiveness Prayer, once silently and once aloud.

4. Scan the Emotional Trigger List on pages 9–14.

5. Write out the 12 Forgiveness Statements for each day's topic on thinking, judging, and believing in your Forgiveness Journal (Days 1–18). Write your Forgiveness Letters (Days 19–21).

6. Perform your Pro EFT™ Forgiveness Tapping Sequences.

7. Process thoughts and feelings consciously through your Forgiveness Journal Reflections.

8. Listen to the *Gratitude Meditation*.

9. Complete the day's practice in quiet reflection or with meditative music.

10. Be sure to do something good for yourself today!

I Forgive Myself for Judging My Relationship with Money

Today's Forgiveness Practice is about forgiving the things we think, believe, and judge about money, wealth, and prosperity in all of its forms. In *The Abundance Book,* John Randolph Price writes that money is a function of **M**y **O**wn **N**atural **E**nergy **Y**ield. In essence, whatever we hold in our minds and hearts will either enhance or obstruct our ability to receive—not just money but all that we desire.

Forgiveness opens the mind and heart, eliminates childhood patterns and beliefs, and increases our chances to receive without doing anything. Today you are encouraged to recall all the stories, myths, instructions, and beliefs you hold about money. Forgive them all and open yourself to receive more than you ever believed or dreamed was possible.

> FORGIVENESS . . . INCREASES OUR CHANCES TO RECEIVE WITHOUT DOING ANYTHING.

A Prayer of Forgiveness

I now consciously and willingly call forth the Holy Spirit and the consciousness of Higher Mind I Am, into every atom, every molecule, every cell, every tissue, every organ, every muscle, and every living system in my being; asking to have transformed every energy, every pattern, every belief, every program, every idea, every attitude, every perception, every expectation, every intention, and every behavior and motivation related to money, wealth, and abundance, bringing them into alignment with the perfect will of God.

I now consciously and willingly call forth the Holy Spirit and the consciousness of the Higher Mind I Am, into every atom, every molecule, every cell, every tissue, every organ, every muscle, and every living system in my being; asking to have transformed every energy, every pattern, every belief, every program, every idea, every attitude, every perception, every expectation, every intention, and every behavior and motivation related to money, bringing them into alignment with the perfect peace and love of God.

For this I am so grateful!

And so it is!

—Excerpted from *Every Day I Pray*

THE FORGIVENESS

DAY 10
JOURNAL WORK

I FORGIVE
MY RELATIONSHIP
WITH MONEY

– I Forgive My Mind for Thinking –

EXAMPLE

I forgive my mind for thinking I should be more financially secure than I am now.

I forgive my mind for thinking money is

_____

_____

I forgive my mind for thinking money is not

_____

_____

I forgive my mind for thinking without money I cannot

_____

_____

I forgive my mind for thinking without money I will not

_____

_____

– I Forgive Myself for Judging –

EXAMPLE

I forgive myself for judging money as the root of all evil.

I forgive myself for judging money as

_____

_____

I forgive myself for judging money as

_____

_____

I forgive myself for judging money as

_____

_____

I forgive myself for judging money as

_____

_____

– I Forgive Myself for Believing –

EXAMPLE

I forgive myself for believing that I should have saved more money instead of helping my children.

I forgive myself for believing
_____
_____

I forgive myself for not believing
_____
_____

I forgive myself for believing that it was wrong for me to consider
_____
_____

I forgive myself for believing it was wrong for me to want
_____
_____

– Tapping Sequence –

BONUS TAPPING SCRIPT DAY 10:
"I FORGIVE MY RELATIONSHIP WITH MONEY"

Identify the Issue and Rate the Intensity Level

After writing out your 12 Forgiveness Statements for Day 10, the specific money forgiveness issue(s) that you want to work on are becoming increasingly clear. Give the issue a name. Now on a scale of 0 to 10, where 0 represents "complete freedom from disturbing thoughts" and 10 represents "these thoughts are driving me crazy," rate the intensity of the thoughts, judgments, and beliefs you have about your relationship with money.

Clearing Resistance/The Reversal Statement

The Reversal Statement neutralizes any subconscious resistance you have to releasing any thoughts, judgments, and beliefs you have about your relationship with money. It acknowledges your resistance and moves you forward anyway.

Since money is one of the greatest societal measures of status and security, our relationship to the energy of money cannot be taken for granted without being subject to a very high price. This is what we are all still learning from the aftershock of the 2008 U. S. financial crisis.

Use the Reversal Statement provided below (or one that you've written yourself) and repeat it three times while tapping continuously on the Karate Chop point.

- Even though I'm stuck in the false belief that I can't have money, and there's no way out, I deeply and profoundly love and accept myself.

THE SET-UP STATEMENT

The Set-Up Statement helps you focus on the issue that you'll be addressing during your tapping session.

Choose one of the Set-Up Statements below (or use one that you've written yourself) and repeat it three times while tapping continuously on the Karate Chop point.

- Even though part of me believes it's hard to make money and I can't figure out why it has to be that way, I love myself totally and unconditionally.

- Even though there is never enough and I can't seem to change my relationship with money despite my wanting to, I love myself and accept how I feel.

- Even though I always work too hard to get money and I'm never paid fairly—maybe because I haven't really earned it or maybe I don't deserve it—I choose to love and accept myself anyway.

Shake your hands out and have a few sips of water. Take a deep breath through your nose. Release the breath slowly and softly through your mouth, making the sound "Ahhhhh" as you do so.

TAPPING SEQUENCE: ROUNDS 1 THROUGH 3

For Tapping Rounds 1 through 3, tap 7 times on each of the 10 meridian points while repeating the Tapping Script that follows, or create your own script using the Forgiveness Statement entries from your daily journal work as your reminder phrases. Using your own personal Forgiveness Statements will keep you laser-focused on your tapping intention as different dimensions of your healing process unfold.

ROUND I

Tap 7 times on each meridian point while repeating out loud either the statements below or your reminder statements.

Eyebrow:	Making money is hard work!
Side of Eye:	It's hard to get money, and it's hard to keep money.
Under Eye:	I've believed this for so long that it has actually manifested in my life.
Under Nose:	It must mean I haven't really earned it or that I don't deserve it.
Chin:	In order for me to have money, I have to pay a high price.
Collarbone:	Making money always involves some kind of discomfort, challenge, hustle, or struggle.
Underarm:	Lots of people who make lots of money don't work as hard as I do.
Liver:	What if having money and abundance is easy to do?
Wrists:	What if I choose to believe that making, having, and keeping money can be easy?
Crown of Head:	What if having money and abundance is actually in the cards for me?

ROUND 2

Tap 7 times on each meridian point while repeating out loud either the statements below or your reminder statements.

Eyebrow:	Making money is easy? Really? That can't be true!
Side of Eye:	What if I've been holding on to an old distortion?
Under Eye:	What if having money is really about changing how I think?
Under Nose:	What if it's about believing I deserve to have what I desire?
Chin:	What if I need money, and God wants me to have it?
Collarbone:	Everything is energy.
Underarm:	What if money is just energy and I open my mind to the energy of money?
Liver:	Can I accept the truth that God wants me to have money and be abundant?
Wrists:	Is it possible to release the false belief that I am unworthy to receive?
Crown of Head:	Can I release all unconscious resistance to abundance and prosperity?

ROUND 3

Now tap 7 times on each meridian point while repeating out loud either the statements below or your reminder statements.

Eyebrow:	I now choose to release all false beliefs about money from every tissue, cell, and muscle in my body.
Side of Eye:	I am now choosing to have all of the money I need and desire.
Under Eye:	I am no longer afraid of money.
Under Nose:	I am now open to having money come to me effortlessly.
Chin:	I am willing to have money.
Collarbone:	I am willing to receive money.
Underarm:	I now gratefully and joyfully allow more money and prosperity into my life.
Liver:	I am now open to having money to spare and share.
Wrists:	I now expect abundance and everything good to come my way.
Crown of Head:	Money is my friend! I have a terrific and healthy relationship with money.

RECHECK THE INTENSITY LEVEL

Recheck your intensity level on holding unforgiveness about yourself. If the level is at 8 or higher, repeat the entire 3-Round Tapping Sequence outlined in the bonus Tapping Script (or your self-created script.)

If the level is less than 8, tap on a Modified Set-Up Statement, then perform the 10-point Tapping Sequence on the Forgiveness Statements from your daily journal work.

MODIFIED SET-UP STATEMENT

Use the Modified Set-Up Statement below (or use one that you've written yourself) and repeat it three times while tapping continuously on the Karate Chop point.

- Even though I still have some stubborn judgments about myself and some resistance to letting them go, I am willing to let them go, and I love and accept myself totally and unconditionally.

After you complete the Tapping Sequence on your Forgiveness Statements, recheck your intensity level on holding unforgiveness about money.

Depending on your level, continue to repeat the sequence described above until you are at a 0 level of intensity.

_____

_____

_____

_____

_____

_____

_____

_____

_____

_____

_____

_____

_____

_____

The forgiving state of mind is a magnetic power for attracting good.

—CATHERINE PONDER

I Forgive My Job, Work, or Career

Beyond this, there is a world I want.
Forgiveness will take me there.

It is up to me to visualize that there is something else
to hope for, more satisfying, filled with joy, and capable
of offering peace to my mind, and peace in my life.
Beyond the perceived hopelessness there is the bright
and shining world of highest hope, greatest aspiration,
miracles everywhere present because I intentionally
hold only miracles in my mind. As I allow myself
to forgive myself for believing in the hopelessness
of the world, miracles unfold all around me.

—Prayer for *A Course in Miracles Workbook*
Lesson 129

– Forgiveness Friend Story by Caryn Daniels –

Like so many people, I had a strong dislike for my job. I hated the location. I was bored by my daily tasks. I secretly disliked many of the people I worked with, and I disrespected and distrusted my two supervisors. I went to work every day because I had children to feed and rent to pay. It wasn't always like that, however. I started out excited about my position, satisfied with my pay, and looking forward to moving up the ladder of this midsized firm. From watching office politics that led to jockeying for position, being passed over when promotions were available, and experiencing demands on my finances that my paycheck did not cover, I grew into a state of misery. Then I got a pink slip, and my feelings quickly changed.

> MY FRIEND . . .
> TOLD ME
> THAT I HAD BEEN
> UNGRATEFUL AND . . .
> SQUANDERING
> MY GIFTS.

Around the time that my unemployment benefits were coming to an end, a friend took me to task about my attitude regarding work. She reminded me how often I had complained about the conditions and the people. That led to a deeper discussion about what I really wanted to do and why I wasn't doing it. What we eventually uncovered was that I was afraid—afraid to ask for what I wanted, afraid to speak up for myself, afraid that I didn't have what it took to do what I really wanted to do. In response to my fears, I blamed other people for what I considered their failure to acknowledge me. The conversation didn't stop there.

My friend, who was a struggling entrepreneur, told me that I had been ungrateful and that I had been squandering my gifts. You see, she knew that I had struggled going to school at night to get a degree. She also knew that I had taken a job that I didn't want, believing I would not survive doing the work I wanted to do. In the midst of my defending myself, using all of the normal arguments people have for not following their dreams, she landed a serious blow to my argument by saying: "That job kept you fed, clothed, and housed for eight years, and you never once said thank you. You measured what they gave you, devalued yourself in the process, and withheld the best of who you are from the world. Work is not just about getting paid what you're worth. It is about using your gifts, sharing the best of who you are, and using what brings you joy to make someone else's life better." Never in my life had I heard anything like that. At the time, it sounded crazy.

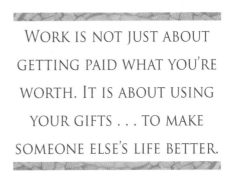

WORK IS NOT JUST ABOUT GETTING PAID WHAT YOU'RE WORTH. IT IS ABOUT USING YOUR GIFTS . . . TO MAKE SOMEONE ELSE'S LIFE BETTER.

I was taught to believe that you work to make money because you need money to live. I was also taught to believe that you need a good education to get a good job, and that your pay should be a demonstration of what you are worth. It never dawned on me that working is the way that we share our gifts with the world and that I should be grateful for the opportunity. I had to admit that I was really afraid to ask for what I thought I was worth and that I was grateful that someone had hired me, even if they didn't pay me enough. And if they didn't pay me enough, why should I be grateful? Well, as my friend put it, "Because you bring your worth with you in your attitude and energy." Wow! Another new idea.

I spent many days thinking about what my friend had said as my unemployment benefits dwindled. Most of it made no sense. What finally opened my eyes and my heart was the part about "using your gifts to make someone else's life better." I had a degree in accounting, but my real joy was painting. I loved to paint and decorate. I never pursued interior decorating as a profession because . . . I was afraid it wouldn't provide me what I needed to survive. I was also afraid that I wouldn't be good enough to compete in that arena. Instead, in order to make money I chose work that did not bring me joy. I also had some reservations about how people would respond to a woman and a mother painting walls to earn a living. I judged that what would bring me joy would also bring me shame and criticism. And who on earth was going to hire a woman to paint their home?

It cost $35 to run an ad in the community paper. I got four calls and took two of the jobs. My first two clients referred me to three others. It has been four years since I brought my first two paintbrushes and six rollers. Now I have three employees and a van. I am enrolled in an interior-decorating course and will graduate in nine months. Had I not spent so much time doing something that made me so miserable, I would have never learned how to appreciate doing what brings me joy. For that I have forgiven myself many times. For the joy and excitement I have going to work every day, I am grateful.

> HAD I NOT SPENT SO MUCH TIME DOING
> SOMETHING THAT MADE ME SO MISERABLE,
> I WOULD HAVE NEVER LEARNED HOW TO
> APPRECIATE DOING WHAT BRINGS ME JOY.

DAILY FORGIVENESS
PROCESS REMINDERS

For a more detailed explanation
of the Daily Forgiveness Process Guidelines, see pages 45–46.

1. Find a quiet place where you will not be disturbed for at least 30 to 60 minutes.

2. Still your mind for at least 5 minutes or listen to the *Stillness Meditation*.

3. Listen to the *Forgiveness Prayer* on the accompanying audio program. Then read the Forgiveness Prayer, once silently and once aloud.

4. Scan the Emotional Trigger List on pages 9–14.

5. Write out the 12 Forgiveness Statements for each day's topic on thinking, judging, and believing in your Forgiveness Journal (Days 1–18). Write your Forgiveness Letters (Days 19–21).

6. Perform your Pro EFT™ Forgiveness Tapping Sequences.

7. Process thoughts and feelings consciously through your Forgiveness Journal Reflections.

8. Listen to the *Gratitude Meditation*.

9. Complete the day's practice in quiet reflection or with meditative music.

10. Be sure to do something good for yourself today!

I Forgive Myself for Judging My Job, Work, or Career

Today's practice is about forgiving our choices, behaviors, and attitudes regarding work and career. Each of us has a gift that we can share with the world. For some, our gifts are sufficient to earn a living. For others, we can use our gifts in one arena while we earn our living in another. Whenever we perform our work to the best of our ability with a Spirit-connected heart, we can transform an act of work into an act of worship. Whether you're in the elevator, the boardroom, or the bathroom—working with others offers an incredible opportunity to reveal our most selfless natures.

> WE CAN TRANSFORM AN ACT OF WORK INTO AN ACT OF WORSHIP.

The key is to be grateful for the scenarios we choose and those in which we find ourselves. The issue is to forgive ourselves for the judgments we have made about the work we do, the people we work with, and the value of what we bring to the work we do. When we do our work with excellence, integrity, and positivity—we can become God's heart and hands in the world.

A Prayer of Forgiveness

Blessed Father God, Holy Mother God:

Today, I thank You for the perfect opportunity to share my gifts with the world. I thank You for opening my mind and heart to the abundant opportunities You have for me to serve Your purpose in my life. I thank You for guiding and directing me into the perfect situation, with the perfect people, who can benefit from all that I can offer. I thank You for opening my eyes and heart to know and embrace my value and worth. I thank You for guiding me into my ideal position with abundant compensation. You promised that if I gave my attention to what You desire for me, You would take care of whatever needs and difficulties confront me. Because You have given me the ability to create my own reality, I now declare that the perfect work situation and my next most appropriate steps are unfolding easily with grace.

For this I am so grateful.

I let it be!

And so it is!

THE FORGIVENESS

DAY 11
JOURNAL WORK

I FORGIVE
MY JOB, WORK,
OR CAREER

– I Forgive My Mind for Thinking –

EXAMPLE

I forgive my mind for thinking that the people I work with are the reason I am miserable at work.

I forgive my mind for thinking my job is _____
_____

I forgive my mind for thinking my job is not _____
_____

I forgive my mind for thinking my career is _____
_____

I forgive my mind for thinking my career is not _____
_____

– I FORGIVE MYSELF FOR JUDGING –

EXAMPLE

I forgive myself for judging the work I do as insignificant and meaningless.

I forgive myself for judging _____

_____

I forgive myself for judging _____

_____

I forgive myself for judging _____

_____

I forgive myself for judging _____

_____

– I Forgive Myself for Believing –

EXAMPLE

I forgive myself for believing I cannot do what I love and make the money I need to thrive in life.

I forgive myself for believing

_____

_____

I forgive myself for believing

_____

_____

I forgive myself for believing

_____

_____

I forgive myself for believing

_____

_____

– TAPPING SEQUENCE –

Review Basic Tapping Sequence Guidelines on pages 53–59.

1. Review each of the day's 12 Forgiveness Statements out loud. This will help you identify the specific aspects of the issue that you want to tap on.

2. Rate the intensity level of any unforgiveness you hold about today's topic on a scale of 1 to 10. Write the number down.

3. Neutralize all subconscious resistance. Repeat a Reversal Statement 3 times while tapping continuously on the Karate Chop point.

4. Focus on the issue you'll be tapping on. Repeat a Set-Up Statement 3 times while tapping continuously on the Karate Chop point.

5. Tap 7 times on each of the 10 meridian points while repeating out loud the key details from the 12 Forgiveness Statements. This process can be modeled on the bonus Tapping Scripts.

6. Recheck the intensity level of any unforgiveness you hold about today's topic. Write the number down. If the level is at 8 or higher, repeat the entire sequence. If the level is less than 8, tap on a Modified Set-Up Statement, then perform the 10-point Tapping Sequence on your 12 Forgiveness Statements until you are at a 0 level of intensity.

– REFLECTIONS –

_____

_____

_____

_____

_____

_____

_____

_____

_____

_____

_____

_____

_____

Forgiving was about letting go and moving on with
my life. In doing so, I had finally set myself free.

—ISABEL LOPEZ, *ISABEL'S HAND-ME-DOWN DREAMS*

I FORGIVE WOMEN

I let forgiveness rest upon all things.
Then forgiveness will be given to me.

The key is in my hand, and I have reached the door.
Father, I thank You for the means to let go
of my angry, hurt thoughts that are in conflict with
Your gift of love. I forgive the thoughts of my mind that
make love conditional. The key is in my hand, and I
have reached the door that allows me to forgive
all things and all people.

—PRAYER FOR *A COURSE IN MIRACLES WORKBOOK*
LESSON 342

She was my big sister; therefore, she should have known better. She should have known I looked up to her and trusted her. She should have known I expected her to protect me and to take my side. She should have known that she was the template I used for my assessment of all women. It's not something we ever discussed, but . . . she should have known, and she didn't. Instead, she betrayed me, broke my heart, and set me up to distrust all women, including myself.

It can be challenging for a woman to trust other women because we are often taught not to trust ourselves. Then we doubt our abilities, choices, and instincts. We can become critical of those women in our midst who surpass our perceived imitations. This criticism can take the form of gossip, betrayal, and unwarranted judgment. Women are also more prone than men to compare themselves to one another. We often measure our value and worth by comparing ourselves to another woman's weight, breast size, complexion, career, talents, financial status, intellect, personal style, marital status, and every other aspect of their lives. Comparison is an act of violence against the self. It also leads to judgments and jealousy of those we deem "better off" than we are. If we aren't the ones doing the comparing, then we're the ones against whom other women measure themselves. In either case, the comparison, judgments, and jealousy can lead to ugly behavior.

Women also have high expectations of themselves—often unreasonably high expectations. When they fail to live up to those expectations, they can and often do project their flaws and failures onto other women. We see in one another the things we cannot see or accept about ourselves. When this happens, we will judge other women for

> COMPARISON IS AN ACT OF VIOLENCE AGAINST THE SELF.

the things we dislike in ourselves. The cycle of comparison, projection, and judgment often results in vicious verbal and emotional attacks among women. This is what happened between my sister and me.

We all have people in our lives who set the mold for how we treat other people and how we expect to be treated. My sister taught me most of what I needed to know about being a woman and what to expect from women. She taught me that women are beautiful and powerful. She taught me that women are sensitive and sensual. Some of this I learned by watching her; some I learned by listening to her. My sister taught me that women can also be cold and mean. She taught me that you can depend on women only sometimes . . . and then, when they fall in love, they will leave you for their love interest.

My sister taught me that certain women friends serve you better than others, and that some women can never be your friends. She rarely explained these things to me because she was my big sister. All I had to do was watch and listen and emulate. I did all of the above until my sister told me that I was mean and cold, sneaky and deceptive, ugly and just plain wrong about everything.

It was one of her friends who started the conversation by saying that I thought I was better than everyone else. I had no idea what she was talking about. My sister filled in the details by criticizing my size and my clothing. She continued by citing my going to college and moving "across town" as evidence that proved that what her friend was saying was valid. That led to a recounting of my failures in relationships, career choices, and financial obligations. The criticism was one thing, the betrayal of my confidences was another. It was, however, the jokes and chiding that tore my heart to shreds. As they continued to banter back and forth, it became clear to me that many of the things I had told my big sister in confidence she had revealed to her friend, who was now using that information as the bat to beat me down. It was hurtful and ugly and a death blow to my relationship with my sister.

> AS I LEARNED TO FORGIVE MY SISTER, I LEARNED TO FORGIVE MYSELF FOR ALL THE TIMES I DID TO OTHER WOMEN WHAT I THOUGHT SHE HAD DONE TO ME.

It was 13 years, our father's death, a divorce (hers not mine), and a bout with breast cancer that taught me I had to forgive her. When I saw her looking frail and bald, I realized that no matter what, she was still my big sister, and

I missed being connected to her. In talking to her, I realized all the women in my life whom I had discounted and disconnected from because of our relationship.

As we talked for the first time in many years, I came to understand that for her, what she had done had no meaning. She thought she was correcting me. She had no idea she was judging me. She thought I was upset because of what her friend had said and, more important, she had done to me what she perceived had been done to her by so many other women, including our mother. Like I said, we all have people in our lives who set the mold for how we treat others and how we expect to be treated by them. As I learned to forgive my sister, I learned to forgive myself for all the times I did to other women what I thought she had done to me.

DAILY FORGIVENESS PROCESS REMINDERS

*For a more detailed explanation
of the Daily Forgiveness Process Guidelines, see pages 45–46.*

1. Find a quiet place where you will not be disturbed for at least 30 to 60 minutes.

2. Still your mind for at least 5 minutes or listen to the *Stillness Meditation*.

3. Listen to the *Forgiveness Prayer* on the accompanying audio program. Then read the Forgiveness Prayer, once silently and once aloud.

4. Scan the Emotional Trigger List on pages 9–14.

5. Write out the 12 Forgiveness Statements for each day's topic on thinking, judging, and believing in your Forgiveness Journal (Days 1–18). Write your Forgiveness Letters (Days 19–21).

6. Perform your Pro EFT™ Forgiveness Tapping Sequences.

7. Process thoughts and feelings consciously through your Forgiveness Journal Reflections.

8. Listen to the *Gratitude Meditation*.

9. Complete the day's practice in quiet reflection or with meditative music.

10. Be sure to do something good for yourself today!

I Forgive Myself for Judging Women

Today's practice is about clearing and releasing the hurts, wounds, and judgments you may hold about or against women. Our experience and expectations of women begins with our mothers. Chances are if we have any judgments about our mothers, they will extend to other women. If you are a woman, it is also important to consider the judgments that you hold about yourself. More often than not, these can and will be projected onto other women.

In our everyday experience we are sure to encounter people, both men and women, who simply behave badly. In order to heal from these encounters, it's important that we carefully examine our own projections and judgments. More often than not, the things we detest and judge in others are a reflection of the things we cannot accept about ourselves. The impact of a lack of self-acceptance is intensified in the relationships between and among women.

> THE THINGS WE DETEST AND JUDGE IN OTHERS ARE A REFLECTION OF THE THINGS WE CANNOT ACCEPT ABOUT OURSELVES.

A Prayer of Forgiveness

Dear God:

Teach me to accept myself so that I will accept all women.

Teach me to appreciate myself so that I will appreciate all women.

Teach me to honor myself so that I will honor all women.

Teach me to respect myself so that I will respect all women.

Teach me to trust myself so that I will trust all women.

Teach me to love myself so that I will love all women.

Teach me to forgive myself so that I will forgive all women.

I open my heart.

I forgive.

I let it be!

And so it is!

THE FORGIVENESS

DAY 12
JOURNAL WORK

I Forgive
Women

– I Forgive My Mind for Thinking –

EXAMPLE

I forgive my mind for thinking women are out to take advantage of me.

I forgive my mind for thinking women are _____

_____

I forgive my mind for thinking women are not _____

_____

I forgive my mind for thinking women always _____

_____

I forgive my mind for thinking women never _____

_____

– I FORGIVE MYSELF FOR JUDGING –

EXAMPLE

I forgive myself for judging women as stupid when it comes to choosing men.

I forgive myself for judging women as _____

_____

I forgive myself for judging women as not _____

_____

I forgive myself for judging women for _____

_____

I forgive myself for judging women for not _____

_____

– I Forgive Myself for Believing –

EXAMPLE

I forgive myself for believing that all women are sneaky and cannot be trusted.

I forgive myself for believing women should

_____

I forgive myself for believing women should not

_____

I forgive myself for believing women always

_____

I forgive myself for believing women never

_____

– TAPPING SEQUENCE –

Review Basic Tapping Sequence Guidelines on pages 53–59.

1. Review each of the day's 12 Forgiveness Statements out loud. This will help you identify the specific aspects of the issue that you want to tap on.

2. Rate the intensity level of any unforgiveness you hold about today's topic on a scale of 1 to 10. Write the number down.

3. Neutralize all subconscious resistance. Repeat a Reversal Statement 3 times while tapping continuously on the Karate Chop point.

4. Focus on the issue you'll be tapping on. Repeat a Set-Up Statement 3 times while tapping continuously on the Karate Chop point.

5. Tap 7 times on each of the 10 meridian points while repeating out loud the key details from the 12 Forgiveness Statements. This process can be modeled on the bonus Tapping Scripts.

6. Recheck the intensity level of any unforgiveness you hold about today's topic. Write the number down. If the level is at 8 or higher, repeat the entire sequence. If the level is less than 8, tap on a Modified Set-Up Statement, then perform the 10-point Tapping Sequence on your 12 Forgiveness Statements until you are at a 0 level of intensity.

- REFLECTIONS -

_____

_____

_____

_____

_____

_____

_____

_____

_____

_____

_____

_____

_____

I can have peace of mind only when I forgive rather than judge.

—GERALD JAMPOLSKY

I Forgive Men

Let me not bind Your son with laws I made.
He is not bound to me except by my beliefs about him.

My only function is to forgive my beliefs that bind me
in the time-space body to pain. I am not bound.
I am free the moment I let go of the false beliefs,
the foolish false beliefs about what I am and who I am;
about what they are and who they are.
My only function is to forgive what I thought
was allowing love to takes its place.

—PRAYER FOR *A COURSE IN MIRACLES WORKBOOK*
LESSON 227

— Forgiveness Story by Iyanla Vanzant —

In spite of all of my misgivings and apprehensions, I really thought we were moving along quite nicely. We had known each other for many years before we became sexual and intimate. We had a healthy respect for each other's space and responsibilities as professionals. We had a great time together walking, talking, laughing, and doing simple things like popping popcorn and eating it while lying in bed. It felt really good to me, and I thought it felt the same for him. Boy, was I wrong! Without warning or provocation, three years into my first healthy relationship, he packed up and left, stating, "I am not the man for you." That was it. No further explanation was offered. Quite frankly, none was required. He was a man! They all lie, cheat, take what they want, and leave you scratching your head, bewildered and brokenhearted. I just thought he was different. I wanted him to be different. It hurt my feelings that he wasn't different, and I was mad as hell that I didn't see it coming.

I have spent the majority of my adult life trying to figure out who to be, how to be, and what to be to keep a man interested and committed in a relationship. I have used food as a way to his stomach and heart. I have been a warm and welcoming, ever-available sexual partner. I've been aloof and hard to catch. I've been coy and demure, helpless and dependent, independent and powerful—none of which has worked. I have asked them what they wanted. I have heard that what he wanted was me. That lasted only until someone younger, older, smarter, thinner, fatter, or more experienced came along. When that didn't work, I made it up as we went along. To that end, I was deemed to be needy, moody, pushy, bossy, too dependent, too independent, angry, passive, aggressive, or fine but the timing was just not right. By the time I was 45, I determined that they were all crazy, they could not be trusted, and that I was going to live the rest of my life happily with Bob, my "battery-operated boyfriend." Thank God I have close, nonsexual male friends to help me figure it all out.

> THE REASON
> YOU KEEP ATTRACTING
> THE ONES WHO LEAVE
> IS BECAUSE YOU EXPECT
> THEM TO DO SO.

Like many women, I had numerous stories of betrayal, disappointment, heartbreak, and vileness that I had hung on the hook of "men." I could have told you chapter and verse what I had done for them and what they had not done for me. I used the sordid details of my stories as an excuse to talk badly about men, judge them, mistrust them, expect little from them, and give of myself begrudgingly as I waited for the axe to fall on my neck. If I were to tell the truth, which is my intention, I would admit that even while I was lying across the bed with my head resting on his chest, licking the butter from the popcorn off of my fingers, there were several persistent thoughts playing in the background of my mind: *I wonder what he really wants from me? This is too good to be true! He must have another woman somewhere. I wonder when and how he is going to leave me.* What my male friends pointed out to me was that if I thought it, he felt it. One went so far as to say, "The reason you keep attracting the ones who leave is because you expect them to do so. You cannot get what you want until you understand what you expect." What the . . . ?! He's a man! He's crazy!

It took me a minute to regroup, but when I thought about what he had said, it began to make sense. I had watched my father, my uncles, my brother, and even my son—only on occasion—treat the women in their lives less than honorably. I watched my stepmother, my aunties, and countless of my sister-friends cry their eyes out over how the men in their lives had betrayed their trust and their love. My observations as a child and a teenager, coupled with my own experiences as a young woman, had left me angry, suspicious, judgmental, and, okay, I'll admit it, bitter. I had loved one man most of

> I FORGIVE MY MIND
> FOR BELIEVING THAT
> WHAT WAS IS WHAT
> ALWAYS HAD TO BE.

life only to have him leave me not once or twice but four times for someone else. I watched my daughter struggle for 15 years in a relationship. I helped my sister pack and sneak away in the night from a 12-year relationship. Somewhere in the back of my mind, not only was I bitter about what I had seen and experienced,

I really did not want any part of it or men again. How was this possible? The thing I was chasing was the thing I didn't want. The thing I yearned for was the very same thing I was afraid of, and it was *their* fault entirely! Men and their nasty, mean, callous ways were totally and completely responsible for the craziness I was experiencing! But then again, if I can only attract what I expect, what was I to do with all of the hurt, sadness, sorrow, anger, and fear that had built up as a result of what I had seen and experienced? Forgive it! Damn!

It ain't easy being a queen or a forgiving soul. *I forgive you, Daddy, for never being there for me and letting me down even when you were there.* To forgive means you must be willing to see things differently in spite of the hurt you feel. *I forgive you, my uncles and cousins and family friends, for violating my innocence with your sexual deviance.* When you spend more time being angry, hurt, and upset about what happened, you pretty much barricade the door of what is possible. *I forgive you, my brother, for abandoning me when I needed you most.* It is impossible for you to express, accept, or demonstrate true unconditional love until you forgive those who did not know how to love. *I forgive you, women in my life, you who stayed in pain longer than it was necessary or productive to do so.* Once you become willing to let it all go, God will open a new space in your heart and rewire your brain to know, receive, and express love in healthy ways. *I forgive myself for believing that what I made up about who they were is the truth I had to live with for years of my life.* Forgiveness is not an easy chore to undertake, nor is it for the weak. *I forgive you, God, for leaving me out here to figure out all of this on my own.* Yet forgiveness is the daily minimum requirement for a healthy, fulfilling, and meaningful life. *I forgive my mind for believing that what was is what always has to be.*

DAILY FORGIVENESS
PROCESS REMINDERS

*For a more detailed explanation
of the Daily Forgiveness Process Guidelines, see pages 45–46.*

1. Find a quiet place where you will not be disturbed for at least 30 to 60 minutes.

2. Still your mind for at least 5 minutes or listen to the *Stillness Meditation.*

3. Listen to the *Forgiveness Prayer* on the accompanying audio program. Then read the Forgiveness Prayer, once silently and once aloud.

4. Scan the Emotional Trigger List on pages 9–14.

5. Write out the 12 Forgiveness Statements for each day's topic on thinking, judging, and believing in your Forgiveness Journal (Days 1–18). Write your Forgiveness Letters (Days 19–21).

6. Perform your Pro EFT™ Forgiveness Tapping Sequences.

7. Process thoughts and feelings consciously through your Forgiveness Journal Reflections.

8. Listen to the *Gratitude Meditation.*

9. Complete the day's practice in quiet reflection or with meditative music.

10. Be sure to do something good for yourself today!

I Forgive Myself for Judging Men

Today is about forgiving men. If you are a man, you may need to forgive your father, brother, or another male figure who has caused hurt, harm, or disappointment in your life. If you are a woman, you may need to forgive those whom you have loved or those who refused to love you; those who have hurt you, shamed you, and abandoned you; or those who left you scarred or wounded. In our world, masculine energy—represents authority, power, and strength. When we have distorted and painful images of men and masculinity, more often than not we find ourselves in dysfunctional relationships with all forms of power and authority. This means that when we need it most, our strength wanes. Open yourself to consider the glorious possibilities that lie just beyond how you have seen, held, and related to the masculine energy of the Creator that is embodied in all men.

> FORGIVE THE MEN YOU HAVE LOVED OR THOSE WHO REFUSED TO LOVE YOU.

A Prayer of Forgiveness

Dear God:

Today I ask for and open myself to receiving healing and restoration of my mind, my heart, and all of my relationships with men. I confess that I have not always been kind or loving toward men. I confess that I have held judgments about men and against men. I confess that I have allowed unkind, unloving, judgmental thoughts and beliefs to infect my relationships with men. For this, I ask for and accept Your forgiveness, and I forgive myself.

Today, I ask that my heart and mind be opened so that I will accept all men as Your sons and my brothers. I ask that You create in me a clean heart and renew a right spirit within me so that my divine relationship with all men will be restored. I ask for the will to forgive and move forward in love.

I lay down my weapons.

I open my heart.

I forgive.

I let it be!

And so it is!

THE FORGIVENESS

DAY 13
JOURNAL WORK

I Forgive Men

– I Forgive My Mind for Thinking –

EXAMPLE

I forgive my mind for thinking men will always abuse and disappoint me.

I forgive my mind for thinking men are _____

_____

I forgive my mind for thinking men are not _____

_____

I forgive my mind for thinking men always _____

_____

I forgive my mind for thinking men never _____

_____

– I Forgive Myself for Judging –

EXAMPLE

I forgive myself for judging all men as being self-centered and irresponsible.

I forgive myself for judging men as

_____

_____

I forgive myself for judging men as not

_____

_____

I forgive myself for judging men for

_____

_____

I forgive myself for judging men for not

_____

_____

– I FORGIVE MYSELF FOR BELIEVING –

EXAMPLE

I forgive myself for believing it is not safe for me to trust the men I work with.

I forgive myself for believing men should _____

_____

I forgive myself for believing men should not _____

_____

I forgive myself for believing men always _____

_____

I forgive myself for believing men never _____

_____

– TAPPING SEQUENCE –

Review Basic Tapping Sequence Guidelines on pages 53–59.

1. Review each of the day's 12 Forgiveness Statements out loud. This will help you identify the specific aspects of the issue that you want to tap on.

2. Rate the intensity level of any unforgiveness you hold about today's topic on a scale of 1 to 10. Write the number down.

3. Neutralize all subconscious resistance. Repeat a Reversal Statement 3 times while tapping continuously on the Karate Chop point.

4. Focus on the issue you'll be tapping on. Repeat a Set-Up Statement 3 times while tapping continuously on the Karate Chop point.

5. Tap 7 times on each of the 10 meridian points while repeating out loud the key details from the 12 Forgiveness Statements. This process can be modeled on the bonus Tapping Scripts.

6. Recheck the intensity level of any unforgiveness you hold about today's topic. Write the number down. If the level is at 8 or higher, repeat the entire sequence. If the level is less than 8, tap on a Modified Set-Up Statement, then perform the 10-point Tapping Sequence on your 12 Forgiveness Statements until you are at a 0 level of intensity.

– REFLECTIONS –

_____

_____

_____

_____

_____

_____

_____

_____

_____

_____

_____

_____

_____

_____

You cannot forgive just once, forgiveness is a daily practice.
—SONIA RUMZI

I FORGIVE MY PARTNER/EX-PARTNER

I want the peace of God.
The peace of God is everything I want.

The peace of God is my one goal; the aim of all my living,
the end I seek, my purpose and my function and my life.
An unpeaceful mind cannot hear God. Any unpeaceful
feeling is the indicator that what I am thinking is forgivable.
Only false ideas disturb my mind, obstructing my natural
peace. Let me remember I am not threatened by what
I see, but by minds whose thoughts are
the images I perceive.

—PRAYER FOR *A COURSE IN MIRACLES WORKBOOK*
LESSON 227

– Forgiveness Friend Story by Almasi Wilcots –

My lesson in forgiveness came when I chose to leave a 23-year marriage. For more years than I care to admit, I would move through my days making every possible effort at being wife and mother of the year. I worked long hours as the cook, housekeeper, laundress, driver, handywoman, and, of course, primary caregiver for the children. I felt like I was dying inside while acting like everything was all right. I blamed him, the husband-father, for everything! Looking back, I realize it was I who overstayed my welcome. I was complete with the relationship six months into the marriage, but I convinced myself that I had to stay because we had a dream that we wanted to realize, although his dream and my dream were completely different.

Then I told myself I had to stay for the children. I had five of them along the way. They, I told myself, needed the love and security of having a father and an intact family. The truth is, more often than not I felt depleted and powerless because I gave him all of my power. I gave him the power to choose, to change, and to do what felt right for me. He made all of the choices, which made me mad. He decided the direction for our family and finances, which was a continuous source of frustration for me. When it came to most things regarding the children and our family, there was only one way to be considered—his way! I went along with it all until I felt like I couldn't breathe.

When I found the strength and courage to leave, I left everything and everyone. I left him, the children, the house, and the bank account. I left with not much more than I had on my back. I guess you could say that I was angry, but that would be the nice way to say it. I just wanted to breathe and live and make some choices for my life and myself. I wanted to find new ways to spend my time.

After doing all of this for a very short time, I began to feel alive again. I began to feel as if I had some freedom and some control in my life. Boy, was I mistaken! As the days and weeks passed, I found myself still blaming him for most of what went wrong. When things didn't go the way I wanted, I blamed him. When my plans did not seem to come together, I blamed him. It didn't take me long to realize that he was still the center of my life. In fact, he was still very much in control of what I did and how I did it. I needed HELP!

> I BLAMED HIM, THE HUSBAND-FATHER FOR EVERYTHING! LOOKING BACK, I REALIZE IT WAS I WHO OVERSTAYED MY WELCOME.

I had heard about this thing called forgiveness. I had seen it mentioned in several self-help books. The only forgiveness I knew about was in the kind reserved for the confessional: "Father, forgive me for I have sinned." In this case, I could not see that what I had done required forgiveness. I just wanted to be free. So instead of forgiveness, I set an intention.

I had learned all about them in a workshop. I put my intention on the bedroom wall so that I would see it and say it every morning and night. It was my intention to experience and express love, peace, joy, fun, and an abundance of every good thing. Little did I know that forgiveness was the direct path to fulfillment of that very intention. I said, "Let me give forgiveness a try."

My mantra became "I forgive everyone for everything." No matter what, "I forgive everyone for everything!" I just said it even though I didn't believe a word . . . at first. Then I wrote the forgiveness statements. Each time I wrote one, he would come up in my mind. How many times do I have to forgive him?! When is he and all of his energy going to vacate the crevices of my mind? The answer came the one day I heard my mind respond, "When you can see the good that came from your relationship and how it prepared you for where you are today." *Wow!*

> HOW MANY TIMES DO I HAVE TO FORGIVE HIM?! WHEN IS HE AND ALL OF HIS ENERGY GOING TO VACATE THE CREVICES OF MY MIND?

As I thought about it and allowed myself to feel my own sorrow and sadness, my thoughts about and my experience of my ex-husband shifted. It didn't happen overnight. Instead, it was slow, gradual, and thorough. Each day I thought of something

I could be grateful about during my time with him. As resistant and reluctant as I had been to give him credit for anything, I really began to appreciate him for all the lessons he taught me and the blessings I received during our marriage. Today, not only can I say I love him, I truly want nothing but the very best for him. He has a very special place in my heart. Forgiveness was the key. Forgiveness = Peace + Love + Joy. And you know what? The best gift of all was realizing that my ex really didn't do anything to me. God was always in control, and so was I.

FORGIVENESS = PEACE + LOVE + JOY.

DAILY FORGIVENESS
PROCESS REMINDERS

*For a more detailed explanation
of the Daily Forgiveness Process Guidelines, see pages 45–46.*

1. Find a quiet place where you will not be disturbed for at least 30 to 60 minutes.

2. Still your mind for at least 5 minutes or listen to the *Stillness Meditation.*

3. Listen to the *Forgiveness Prayer* on the accompanying audio program. Then read the Forgiveness Prayer, once silently and once aloud.

4. Scan the Emotional Trigger List on pages 9–14.

5. Write out the 12 Forgiveness Statements for each day's topic on thinking, judging, and believing in your Forgiveness Journal (Days 1–18). Write your Forgiveness Letters (Days 19–21).

6. Perform your Pro EFT™ Forgiveness Tapping Sequences.

7. Process thoughts and feelings consciously through your Forgiveness Journal Reflections.

8. Listen to the *Gratitude Meditation.*

9. Complete the day's practice in quiet reflection or with meditative music.

10. Be sure to do something good for yourself today!

I Forgive Myself for Judging My Partner/Ex-Partner

Today's forgiveness practice is about releasing and healing all grievances we hold against our current or a past intimate partner. The challenge with those whom we love is that they are the only ones who can get close enough to us to cause us heartbreak. They are also the ones who come into our lives to teach us the most powerful lessons. Unfortunately, it is normal to get stuck on the heartbreak, and in doing so miss the lessons.

> WHAT PART OF YOURSELF CAN YOU SEE IN YOUR PARTNER/ EX-PARTNER?

As you move through today's practice, give yourself permission to tell the low-down, dirty truth about what you are thinking, feeling, and believing. What part of yourself can you see in your partner/ ex-partner? And are you willing to forgive it in you? *Love brings up everything unlike itself.* This means the deeper you love someone, the more unloving parts of yourself will be revealed.

A Prayer of Forgiveness

Dear God:

Once again, I lay my weapons down. This time, I really mean it. This time, I really open my heart. This time, I really surrender my hurts and judgments. This time, I ask for and open myself to know the part of myself that is being revealed in the behavior of my partner/ex-partner. I ask to know and see it. I ask to acknowledge and heal it. I forgive myself for making this so hard on myself and for blaming someone else for the pain I have endured.

I rest in thee.

I let it be.

And so it is.

THE FORGIVENESS

DAY 14
JOURNAL WORK

I Forgive My
Partner/Ex-Partner

– I Forgive My Mind for Thinking –

EXAMPLE

I forgive my mind for thinking that my wife is not worth my time or energy.

I forgive my mind for thinking
_____

is
_____

I forgive my mind for thinking
_____

is not
_____

I forgive my mind for thinking
_____

has always
_____

I forgive my mind for thinking
_____

will never
_____

– I Forgive Myself for Judging –

EXAMPLE

I forgive myself for judging my ex-husband for not having a better relationship with our children.

I forgive myself for judging _____

for _____

I forgive myself for judging _____

for not _____

I forgive myself for judging _____

about _____

I forgive myself for judging _____

should _____

– I Forgive Myself for Believing –

EXAMPLE

I forgive myself for believing that my ex-partner, and not my choices, are responsible for my unhappiness.

I forgive myself for believing

should

I forgive myself for believing

should not

I forgive myself for believing

has not

I forgive myself for believing

cannot

– TAPPING SEQUENCE –

Review Basic Tapping Sequence Guidelines on pages 53–59.

1. Review each of the day's 12 Forgiveness Statements out loud. This will help you identify the specific aspects of the issue that you want to tap on.

2. Rate the intensity level of any unforgiveness you hold about today's topic on a scale of 1 to 10. Write the number down.

3. Neutralize all subconscious resistance. Repeat a Reversal Statement 3 times while tapping continuously on the Karate Chop point.

4. Focus on the issue you'll be tapping on. Repeat a Set-Up Statement 3 times while tapping continuously on the Karate Chop point.

5. Tap 7 times on each of the 10 meridian points while repeating out loud the key details from the 12 Forgiveness Statements. This process can be modeled on the bonus Tapping Scripts.

6. Recheck the intensity level of any unforgiveness you hold about today's topic. Write the number down. If the level is at 8 or higher, repeat the entire sequence. If the level is less than 8, tap on a Modified Set-Up Statement, then perform the 10-point Tapping Sequence on your 12 Forgiveness Statements until you are at a 0 level of intensity.

– REFLECTIONS –

_____

_____

_____

_____

_____

_____

_____

_____

_____

_____

_____

_____

With forgiveness, your victim identity dissolves, and
your true power emerges—the power of Presence.
Instead of blaming the darkness, you bring in the light.

—ECKHART TOLLE,
A NEW EARTH: AWAKENING TO YOUR LIFE'S PURPOSE

I Forgive My Brother/Sister

I trust my brothers, who are one with me.

Everything I do to my brothers who are one with me,
I do to myself. Everything that I do to myself, I do
unto my brothers. No part of You is individualized,
different, special, or separate, but All One Self.
What could give me greater peace than to unify
with every aspect of what you have created?
Today I choose to trust my brothers
who are one in love with You.

—PRAYER FOR *A COURSE IN MIRACLES WORKBOOK*
LESSON 181

– Forgiveness Friend Story by Rev. Beverly Saunders Biddle –

Over 35 years—hard, dark years, I had been harboring anger and resentment against my father and brother. For my dad, I was enraged for what I remembered as an unstable home life due to his alcoholism. For my brother, it was because he was not available to my parents or me during their illnesses and ultimate transitions. For these two very important men in my life, forgiveness was not something I offered because, quite frankly, I didn't think they deserved it. Thank God for another thought!

As a child, I felt embarrassed for a good portion of the time because of my father's drinking. We moved a lot because holding a job was hard for him. And there were many instances when he would stumble drunk in the street, or take me shopping and never buy the things he promised, or show up to my school in front of all of my friends. Even as an adult, I felt the same embarrassment when he could hardly walk me down the aisle at my wedding. These were very painful memories that I used as a weapon against my father in my own heart and mind. These weapons robbed me of what could have been a beautiful relationship with him and other men in my life.

MY BROTHER WAS MY SURROGATE FATHER. I TRUSTED HIM.

I had always looked up to my brother as a straight-A student, a musician, and an athlete. When I was an adolescent, my parents separated. For the first few very difficult years, my brother was my surrogate father. I trusted him. I depended on him to keep me in line and to make me feel safe. When my aged parents were in failing health, and when they both passed on, I never thought he wouldn't be there for them and for me. I was mistaken.

He was nowhere to be found. I felt betrayed, abandoned, and disappointed that my hero turned out to be a total flake. At least he was in my mind. I vowed never to forgive him for not being who I needed and wanted him to be in my life. How dare he!

> PEOPLE DO THE BEST THEY CAN WITH WHAT THEY HAVE IN ANY GIVEN MOMENT.

Today, I am amazed at the ways I justified my anger and self-righteousness about the man who gave me life and the one who did his best to teach me how to live it. I told myself that both of them had failed miserably at living up to my expectations of a father and an older brother. Of course, in my mind and in my heart, it was all about me and what I felt I did not get from them. Then my marriage as well as other pieces and parts of my life fell apart. From my broken places I recognized the same in my father and brother. From my own sense of darkness I saw the light they actually were in my life. Oh my God! Had I really held them hostage to my anger for more than 35 years? You bet I did! And I knew that forgiveness was the only hostage negotiator clever or savvy enough to free us all.

Practicing forgiveness shifted my perspective, my life, and the vital signs of my family relationships. Not until I began forgiving my father and brother was I able to see things from their perspectives. Forgiving these two important men in my life for what I had judged as offenses against me opened my heart in ways I never knew were possible. As I stopped giving lip service to forgiveness and really put it into practice, I learned that people do the best they can with what they have in any given moment.

Both of these men, whom I loved dearly, were veterans who had served this country and lost pieces and parts of themselves in the process. My father, a black man, served during World War II, at a time when he was forced to enter certain establishments through back doors in his own country. He served again in the Korean War, only to come home and have great difficulty in finding a job after serving his country for 23 years. My brother served in Vietnam. It was a war about which two Oscar-winning movies have been made. I can only imagine the horrors he saw and endured that would push any rational thinking man over the edge.

When I was able to see life through their eyes, I was able to make a shift within my own consciousness. Not until I became willing to acknowledge what they had lived through and lived with as men was I able to find, hold, and see them with compassion. Compassion, one of my greatest teachers, allowed me to truly

PRACTICING FORGIVENESS SHIFTED MY PERSPECTIVE, MY LIFE, AND THE VITAL SIGNS OF MY FAMILY RELATIONSHIPS.

forgive them in order to free myself. With a newfound depth of compassion guiding me and a heart full of love, I moved beyond lip service in order to dive into forgiveness. Much to my surprise, as I set them free, I was able to forgive myself for the judgments I had made about them. I now hold them in a loving space in my heart and honor them as my ancestors who love me and guide me each day.

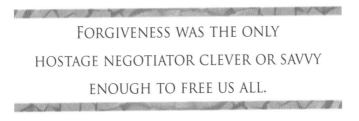

FORGIVENESS WAS THE ONLY
HOSTAGE NEGOTIATOR CLEVER OR SAVVY
ENOUGH TO FREE US ALL.

DAILY FORGIVENESS PROCESS REMINDERS

*For a more detailed explanation
of the Daily Forgiveness Process Guidelines, see pages 45–46.*

1. Find a quiet place where you will not be disturbed for at least 30 to 60 minutes.

2. Still your mind for at least 5 minutes or listen to the *Stillness Meditation.*

3. Listen to the *Forgiveness Prayer* on the accompanying audio program. Then read the Forgiveness Prayer, once silently and once aloud.

4. Scan the Emotional Trigger List on pages 9–14.

5. Write out the 12 Forgiveness Statements for each day's topic on thinking, judging, and believing in your Forgiveness Journal (Days 1–18). Write your Forgiveness Letters (Days 19–21).

6. Perform your Pro EFT™ Forgiveness Tapping Sequences.

7. Process thoughts and feelings consciously through your Forgiveness Journal Reflections.

8. Listen to the *Gratitude Meditation.*

9. Complete the day's practice in quiet reflection or with meditative music.

10. Be sure to do something good for yourself today!

I Forgive Myself for Judging My Brother/Sister

Today's forgiveness practice is about forgiving judgments we hold and the hurts we may have attached to our siblings. In many sibling relationships there are three evil elements: comparison, jealousy, and ridicule. What siblings say and do to one another often can cut deep and leave scars. On the other hand, what siblings do *not* say and refuse to do for one another often cuts deeper and leaves profound wounds.

Whether you are the elder, the junior, or somewhere in the middle, there is nothing more precious and supportive than a close relationship with a sibling. When there is a breakdown in the relationship between siblings, the pain and dysfunction can affect and infect the entire family. Today's practice of healing broken sibling relationships may also help you heal similar issues in your friendships.

> IN MANY SIBLING RELATIONSHIPS THERE ARE THREE EVIL ELEMENTS: COMPARISON, JEALOUSY, AND RIDICULE.

A Prayer of Forgiveness

Dear God:

I am willing to change my mind. I am willing to experience a change of heart. I am willing to change my perception of myself. I am willing to change my perception of my brother/sister. I am willing to change what I think and why I think it. I am willing to change what I say and how I say it. I am willing to change my attitudes, my opinions, my habitual responses, my limited perceptions, the silent agreements, the family patterns, everything and anything I think or hold in my heart that will restore peace and harmony in my relationship with my brother/sister. I now consciously and willing ask the Holy Spirit of Your love to change every every cell, every tissue, every organ, every muscle, and every living system within my being in order to transform my relationship with my brother/sister. I now consciously and willingly ask the Holy Spirit to heal every thought, every belief, every program, every expectation, every motivation, and every behavior that has had or may have a negative, unkind, or unloving impact on my relationship with my brother/sister.

I rest in Thee.

I let it be!

And so it is!

THE FORGIVENESS

DAY 15
JOURNAL WORK

I FORGIVE MY BROTHER/SISTER

– I Forgive My Mind for Thinking –

EXAMPLE

I forgive my mind for thinking that my brother is ungrateful.

I forgive my mind for thinking my brother/sister should be

_____

_____

I forgive my mind for thinking my brother/sister should not be

_____

_____

I forgive my mind for thinking my brother/sister is

_____

_____

I forgive my mind for thinking my brother/sister is not

_____

_____

– I Forgive Myself for Judging –

EXAMPLE

I forgive myself for judging my sister for leaving her children at home alone.

I forgive myself for judging my brother/sister for

_____

_____

I forgive myself for judging my brother/sister for not

_____

_____

I forgive myself for judging my brother/sister as

_____

_____

I forgive myself for judging my brother/sister when

_____

_____

– I Forgive Myself for Believing –

EXAMPLE

I forgive myself for believing all the gossip my uncle has told me about my brother.

I forgive myself for believing

_____ about my brother/sister.

I forgive myself for believing

_____ about my brother/sister.

I forgive myself for believing

_____ about my brother/sister.

I forgive myself for believing

_____ about my brother/sister.

– TAPPING SEQUENCE –

Review Basic Tapping Sequence Guidelines on pages 53–59.

1. Review each of the day's 12 Forgiveness Statements out loud. This will help you identify the specific aspects of the issue that you want to tap on.

2. Rate the intensity level of any unforgiveness you hold about today's topic on a scale of 1 to 10. Write the number down.

3. Neutralize all subconscious resistance. Repeat a Reversal Statement 3 times while tapping continuously on the Karate Chop point.

4. Focus on the issue you'll be tapping on. Repeat a Set-Up Statement 3 times while tapping continuously on the Karate Chop point.

5. Tap 7 times on each of the 10 meridian points while repeating out loud the key details from the 12 Forgiveness Statements. This process can be modeled on the bonus Tapping Scripts.

6. Recheck the intensity level of any unforgiveness you hold about today's topic. Write the number down. If the level is at 8 or higher, repeat the entire sequence. If the level is less than 8, tap on a Modified Set-Up Statement, then perform the 10-point Tapping Sequence on your 12 Forgiveness Statements until you are at a 0 level of intensity.

To forgive does not mean to condone.

—ALLAN LOKOS, *PATIENCE: THE ART OF PEACEFUL LIVING*

I Forgive My
Son/Daughter

I am entrusted with the gifts of God.

The gifts of God are mine, entrusted to my care.
God's trust in me is limitless. I am entrusted with
giving happiness and love, doing God's will on earth.
Only by sharing God's love for me, by loving all
whom I will, I realize I have received
the love of God.

—Prayer for *A Course in Miracles* Workbook
Lesson 335

– Forgiveness Story by Iyanla Vanzant –

She was my baby girl, the last of three. Like every other mother, I thought she was the most adorable baby in the world. She was also a good baby. She slept through most of the night and was never a fussy eater. Her brother and sister helped her to crawl around and stand up early. She started walking the same day her first two teeth showed up. The toddler years were easy. Her adolescence was basically uneventful. Then we hit the teenage years, and all hell broke loose.

No matter what I said, it turned into an argument. She was the first of the three to be openly defiant. I think her siblings were as shocked as I was about the things she said and did. Following in my footsteps, she got pregnant at age 16.

Although she finished high school, my baby girl decided not to go to college. She left home and lived with her boyfriend. I usually heard from her when she had a problem. This meant that there were weeks, sometimes months, when we didn't speak. In her mind, I was wrong . . . about everything. In my mind, she was a disappointment. By the time she was 30 I realized that one of us needed to get off our position and mend the fences or we would miss a lot more of each other's life.

It's always the mother who has to give in. I promise you, I did my best. She was having none of it. I was living in another state when I realized . . . I miss my baby girl.

Like so many parents, I had hopes and dreams and wishes for all of my children. I wanted so much for them and expected so much from them. I also had lots of opinions that I thought they needed to follow. My way was the best way. After all, I am the momma!

As hard as it is to admit, I judged my children as good/bad, right/wrong, respectful/disrespectful based on how well they walked the lines I had drawn. I tried so hard to keep them from failing that I failed to give them what they needed to succeed. These were truths I had to face and deal with.

I had to examine my opinions, judgments, and criticisms of my children; forgive myself; and ask them for forgiveness. More important, I had to see the best in them, no matter what they chose for themselves.

> I TRIED SO HARD TO KEEP THEM FROM FAILING THAT I FAILED TO GIVE THEM WHAT THEY NEEDED TO SUCCEED.

The eldest two were more than amenable. They actually believed I had done the best I could. The baby girl, the one who was most like me, had a much harder time. She was suspicious and still very angry. She still didn't want my input. She was her own woman, with her own way of being and her own life to live. Deeper into forgiveness I went. More judgments did I find. In the end, I realized that the more I forgave myself, the closer we became; and the closer we became, the more judgments I had to forgive. What's a mother to do?

DAILY FORGIVENESS
PROCESS REMINDERS

For a more detailed explanation
of the Daily Forgiveness Process Guidelines, see pages 45–46.

1. Find a quiet place where you will not be disturbed for at least 30 to 60 minutes.

2. Still your mind for at least 5 minutes or listen to the *Stillness Meditation*.

3. Listen to the *Forgiveness Prayer* on the accompanying audio program. Then read the Forgiveness Prayer, once silently and once aloud.

4. Scan the Emotional Trigger List on pages 9–14.

5. Write out the 12 Forgiveness Statements for each day's topic on thinking, judging, and believing in your Forgiveness Journal (Days 1–18). Write your Forgiveness Letters (Days 19–21).

6. Perform your Pro EFT™ Forgiveness Tapping Sequences.

7. Process thoughts and feelings consciously through your Forgiveness Journal Reflections.

8. Listen to the *Gratitude Meditation*.

9. Complete the day's practice in quiet reflection or with meditative music.

10. Be sure to do something good for yourself today!

I Forgive Myself for Judging My Son/Daughter

Today's forgiveness practice is for parents who have judgments and disappointments related to their children, even if they are adults. Parents often have dreams for their children that are not the same as the dreams the children have for themselves. When children strike out on their own in their lives, doing things differently than the parents would do them or advise them to do, it can cause a breakdown in the relationship.

Parents forget that their children, especially adult children, are under no obligation to walk their path. Today's practice offers parents the opportunity to free themselves and their children from customs, traditions, rules, and regulations that may have them bound to dysfunction. Work on each of your children for one complete practice. Don't be afraid to be absolutely honest!

> PARENTS OFTEN HAVE DREAMS FOR THEIR CHILDREN THAT ARE NOT THE SAME AS THE DREAMS THE CHILDREN HAVE FOR THEMSELVES.

A Prayer of Forgiveness

Blessed and Divine Father God, Holy and Merciful Mother God:

Thank You for trusting me with the tasks and duties of being a parent. Thank You for the blessing that my son/daughter is in my life. Thank You for establishing and sustaining a bond of love between us that cannot be broken, that is life-sustaining, that is whole and holy. Today, I ask that You will bless my son's/daughter's mind to be free from all doubts in himself/herself and in You. Bless my son/daughter with a kind heart. I ask that You write Your will upon his/her heart and call it into his/ her mind according to our perfect timing. I ask that You give my son/ daughter courage and wisdom. Give him/her strength. Give him/her the desire to do what is good and right at all times, in all situations, and under all circumstances. Thank You, God, for loving my child even more than I do. Thank You for protecting my child, our child, from all hurt, harm, and danger.

Into Your hands I commit him/her.

I rest in Thee.

I let it be!

And so it is!

THE FORGIVENESS

DAY 16
JOURNAL WORK

*I Forgive My
Son/Daughter*

– I FORGIVE MY MIND FOR THINKING –

EXAMPLE

I forgive my mind for thinking I have somehow failed my children because they have not lived up to my expectations.

I forgive my mind for thinking _____

_____ about my son/daughter.

I forgive my mind for thinking _____

_____ about my son/daughter.

I forgive my mind for thinking _____

_____ about my son/daughter.

I forgive my mind for thinking _____

_____ about my son/daughter.

– I FORGIVE MYSELF FOR JUDGING –

EXAMPLE

I forgive myself for judging my son/daughter for not finishing school and working in dead-end jobs.

I forgive myself for judging my son/daughter for

_____

_____

I forgive myself for judging my son/daughter for not

_____

_____

I forgive myself for judging my son/daughter when

_____

_____

I forgive myself for judging my son/daughter because

_____

_____

– I Forgive Myself for Believing –

EXAMPLE

I forgive myself for believing my son/daughter has dishonored me as a parent.

I forgive myself for believing

_____

about my son/daughter.

I forgive myself for believing

_____

about my son/daughter.

I forgive myself for believing

_____

about my son/daughter.

I forgive myself for believing

_____

about my son/daughter.

– TAPPING SEQUENCE –

Review Basic Tapping Sequence Guidelines on pages 53–59.

1. Review each of the day's 12 Forgiveness Statements out loud. This will help you identify the specific aspects of the issue that you want to tap on.

2. Rate the intensity level of any unforgiveness you hold about today's topic on a scale of 1 to 10. Write the number down.

3. Neutralize all subconscious resistance. Repeat a Reversal Statement 3 times while tapping continuously on the Karate Chop point.

4. Focus on the issue you'll be tapping on. Repeat a Set-Up Statement 3 times while tapping continuously on the Karate Chop point.

5. Tap 7 times on each of the 10 meridian points while repeating out loud the key details from the 12 Forgiveness Statements. This process can be modeled on the bonus Tapping Scripts.

6. Recheck the intensity level of any unforgiveness you hold about today's topic. Write the number down. If the level is at 8 or higher, repeat the entire sequence. If the level is less than 8, tap on a Modified Set-Up Statement, then perform the 10-point Tapping Sequence on your 12 Forgiveness Statements until you are at a 0 level of intensity.

– REFLECTIONS –

_____

_____

_____

_____

_____

_____

_____

_____

_____

_____

_____

_____

_____

_____

Forgiveness says you are given another
chance to make a new beginning.

—Desmond Tutu

I Forgive Others

(Friends or Frenemies, Family, Co-Workers, Bosses, Acquaintances, and Even Strangers)

*I offer only miracles today, for
I would have them be returned to me.*

God's gift is love. Love can only create itself.
Today I choose to give only love because love
is all that I want to receive.

—Prayer for *A Course in Miracles Workbook*
Lesson 335

— Forgiveness Friend Story by Rev. Matthew Cartwright —

I now know that nothing in my life will change until I change the way I see my life and myself. I saw myself as a victim for most of my life. The hurt of my perceived childhood abandonment and social ridicule for being gay led to a life of drugs, alcohol, and sex. Rather than deal with my feelings, I chose to escape all the pain of what "they did to me." I was trapped in a world of hurt, resentment, fear, and pain that left me feeling desperate in a life that didn't make sense. It was this feeling of desperation and loneliness that led me deep into a drug addiction and a series of unhealthy choices from which I contracted HIV.

When I tested positive, I felt shattered and even more broken. After all I had already been through, this was like being hit in the face for no good reason. How could I have let this happen? I knew better! I knew how to protect myself, but I hadn't. In the 1990s, I was a volunteer for several AIDS organizations. I had instructed people about what to do and not to do to avoid the life-altering possibilities of this once-deadly disease. Now I was "one of them." I could no longer pretend that I was better than or less than anyone else. I had to fight for my life. For me, that meant doing the work—the deep, hard work to clean up my mind and my heart as well as my life.

> FORGIVENESS REQUIRES SURRENDER.

When you are a gay man, people judge you. More powerful than the judgments others hurled at me were the resentments I held and direct-ed toward others. It was the depth of my own self-generated pain that led me into the practice of forgiveness. I wanted to be healed not only of the pain I had caused myself but of the perceived pain I thought others had visited upon me. I wonder if people realized the pain they cause with their mean speaking and judgments? I wonder if I realized it? With a life-threat-ening diagnosis hanging over my head, I decided that it didn't matter. Forgiveness, I

> I WONDER IF PEOPLE REALIZED THE PAIN THEY CAUSE WITH THEIR MEAN SPEAKING AND JUDGMENTS?

believed, would wipe the slate clean, giving me a new lease on life. As my forgiveness practice deepened, I found the courage to forgive my mother, my father, and everyone I believed had harmed me. I began to feel better and hopeful until I realized that I had not or could not forgive myself.

It was amazing for me to realize that many of the judgments made about me were the same judgments I held about myself. At the same time I had this underlying well of judgment about others that I could not seem to shake loose. I covered those things well. I was great at acting as if every-thing was okay and I was no longer hurting. As the voices and images of shame and wrongness, anger and resentment swirled in my mind, I felt defeated and unlovable. I eventually convinced myself that my wounds were too powerful for any forgiveness or journal exercise.

Although frustrated and angry, I was determined not to give up on forgiveness or myself. It was then that I discovered a little-known secret about any real forgiveness practice: forgiveness requires surrender. Surrender is a state of mind and being that opens the mind and heart to divine revelation. Deeper than changing the mind or healing the heart, surrender eradicates the thoughts, the emotions, and the energies that keep frustration and anger in place. It was not until I surrendered to God, trusting that no matter what happened or did not happen, God would still love me, that I felt a shift. I let go of thinking that I had done something wrong. I asked to be healed of my shame. I prayed for forgiveness for what I had done, and I forgave myself for believing anyone had done anything to me.

> IT IS ARROGANT OF ME NOT TO FORGIVE MYSELF WHEN GOD FORGIVES ME.

Surrender freed me from the prison of shoulda, coulda, and woulda and ushered me into the realization that there are no victims. Our lives are about choices. The greatest gift of surrender was that it helped me to realize that it is arrogant of me not to forgive myself when God forgives me. It is also harmful not to forgive others when God forgives them.

Surrender and forgiveness make it so much easier to forgive myself when I make a mistake. I now forgive others quickly as well. With each report of my health improving, I recognize the healing power of forgiveness. I see how God has empowered me to live fully. The experience with HIV has changed my relationship with God and the world. It has set me free from the prison of my mind that caused me to judge others and myself.

SURRENDER AND FORGIVENESS
MAKE IT SO MUCH EASIER TO FORGIVE MYSELF
WHEN I MAKE A MISTAKE. I NOW FORGIVE
OTHERS QUICKLY AS WELL.

Daily Forgiveness Process Reminders

For a more detailed explanation
of the Daily Forgiveness Process Guidelines, see pages 45–46.

1. Find a quiet place where you will not be disturbed for at least 30 to 60 minutes.

2. Still your mind for at least 5 minutes or listen to the *Stillness Meditation*.

3. Listen to the *Forgiveness Prayer* on the accompanying audio program. Then read the Forgiveness Prayer, once silently and once aloud.

4. Scan the Emotional Trigger List on pages 9–14.

5. Write out the 12 Forgiveness Statements for each day's topic on thinking, judging, and believing in your Forgiveness Journal (Days 1–18). Write your Forgiveness Letters (Days 19–21).

6. Perform your Pro EFT™ Forgiveness Tapping Sequences.

7. Process thoughts and feelings consciously through your Forgiveness Journal Reflections.

8. Listen to the *Gratitude Meditation*.

9. Complete the day's practice in quiet reflection or with meditative music.

10. Be sure to do something good for yourself today!

I Forgive Myself for Judging Others

(Friends or Frenemies, Family, Co-Workers, Bosses, Acquaintances, and Even Strangers)

Today's forgiveness practice is about forgiving the secret, unspoken, or long-held grievances you may hold about or against the people with whom you interact often. This includes those people in the work or social environment, or even extended family members that you believe have harmed, hurt, dishonored, or disrespected you at one time or another.

You will need to forgive friends whom you don't know how to get rid of or those to whom you have not been willing to speak the truth. Today you can address all the others with whom you may have an unresolved upset. Again, give yourself permission to be radically honest; name names and recall incidents. Make a list and, if necessary, take a day to do the work on each person.

> YOU WILL NEED TO FORGIVE FRIENDS WHOM YOU DON'T KNOW HOW TO GET RID OF OR THOSE TO WHOM YOU HAVE NOT BEEN WILLING TO SPEAK THE TRUTH.

A Prayer of Forgiveness

Precious Lord of My Life and Being:

It is my deepest and most heartfelt desire to be a better me today. I desire to be more of what and who You created me to be today. I desire to create a life and relationships that complement who You are in me. Today, I set my hands to do Your work. I allow my heart and mind to align with Your will, and I come present to each moment, allowing all possibilities to unfold in a manner that honors You. Today, I release all personal judgment and complaints and embrace the beauty and goodness of every experience. I give myself permission to do things differently, in a more loving way. I take authority and dominion over my old habits and patterns so that I will awaken to a new way of thinking, being, and living. I forgive all things, people, and experiences of the past. I take a few moments each hour to offer gratitude to You for allowing a better me to emerge today.

I lay my weapons down

I open my heart to peace today.

I rest in Thee today.

I let it be!

And so it is!

—Rev. Heather Mizell

THE FORGIVENESS

DAY 17
JOURNAL WORK

I Forgive Others

– I Forgive My Mind for Thinking –

EXAMPLE

I forgive my mind for thinking that I have control over what people think about me.

I forgive my mind for thinking that _____

should _____

I forgive my mind for thinking that _____

should not _____

I forgive my mind for thinking that _____

is obligated to _____

I forgive my mind for thinking I am responsible for the _____

of _____

– I Forgive Myself for Judging –

EXAMPLE

I forgive myself for judging the co-workers who have criticized and ridiculed my beliefs.

I forgive myself for judging _____

as _____

I forgive myself for judging _____

as _____

I forgive myself for judging _____

as _____

I forgive myself for judging _____

as _____

– I FORGIVE MYSELF FOR BELIEVING –

EXAMPLE

I forgive myself for believing my boss is being disrespectful for not saying good morning.

I forgive myself for believing

_____

about

_____

I forgive myself for not believing

_____

about

_____

I forgive myself for believing that others

_____

_____

I forgive myself for not believing that others

_____

_____

– TAPPING SEQUENCE –

Review Basic Tapping Sequence Guidelines on pages 53–59.

1. Review each of the day's 12 Forgiveness Statements out loud. This will help you identify the specific aspects of the issue that you want to tap on.

2. Rate the intensity level of any unforgiveness you hold about today's topic on a scale of 1 to 10. Write the number down.

3. Neutralize all subconscious resistance. Repeat a Reversal Statement 3 times while tapping continuously on the Karate Chop point.

4. Focus on the issue you'll be tapping on. Repeat a Set-Up Statement 3 times while tapping continuously on the Karate Chop point.

5. Tap 7 times on each of the 10 meridian points while repeating out loud the key details from the 12 Forgiveness Statements. This process can be modeled on the bonus Tapping Scripts.

6. Recheck the intensity level of any unforgiveness you hold about today's topic. Write the number down. If the level is at 8 or higher, repeat the entire sequence. If the level is less than 8, tap on a Modified Set-Up Statement, then perform the 10-point Tapping Sequence on your 12 Forgiveness Statements until you are at a 0 level of intensity.

– REFLECTIONS –

_____

_____

_____

_____

_____

_____

_____

_____

_____

_____

_____

_____

_____

One forgives to the degree that one loves.

—Francois de La Rochefoucauld

I FORGIVE THE WORLD

This holy instant would I give to You.

Be You in charge. For I will follow You.
Now I train my mind to remember You, forgiving all
that I thought happened. This is my responsibility,
to choose the thoughts I think. And if I need a word
to help me, You will give it to me. If I need a thought,
this You will also give. And if I need stillness and
a tranquil, open mind, these are the gifts
I will receive from You.

—PRAYER FOR *A COURSE IN MIRACLES WORKBOOK*
LESSON 363

FORGIVENESS

I was browsing around on social media, trying to catch up on what people were thinking and feeling about what was going on in the world. There were several really hot topics, and the folks seemed to be heated about their thoughts, feelings, and positions. It was amazing to me that so many people could have so much to say about the same thing and never find a common ground. Then I bumped into the meanness, the name-calling, and what felt to me like total disrespect. *What in the world? Have these people lost their minds?*

There are many things about the world, the people in it, and how they live that are not to my taste or liking. Yet I respect people's right to choose, recognizing that things are changing . . . quickly. The issue for me and perhaps many others is how we address our dislike without dissing other people and their basic human rights. How do we share our experiences, allow our voices to be heard, explore our differences in honorable and respectful ways? I guess it all boils down to this: *How do we stop judging one another in order to create productive change of the things that affect us all?*

Every wrong we find in or about someone is a judgment. When we judge, we invoke the energy of *against-ness* that more often than not leads us to attack. When against-ness is at work, the attack is rarely physical. It is psychological or intellectual. It is emotional. Judgment is harsh and mean and meant to hurt, as if the pain of what we do or say will slap others into our way of believing. Whether we are against the opinion or the position or the behavior of the other people or the situation, the attack is always grounded in a judgment of the wrongness.

Because we can never really know what motivates other people, it's difficult to know for certain that their views, opinions, and behaviors are not valid . . . based on what they know. History, experience, and exposure mold people, and people create the world in which we live.

Our world is what it is because of who we are as individuals living in a collective environment. Whether it is the death penalty, fashion trends, same-sex marriage, religious affiliations, or smoking in bars, we are living the reality that somebody or many somebodies are thinking, feeling, and supporting.

The great writer Henry David Thoreau wrote: "It's not what you look at that matters. It's what you see." If the world is a picture

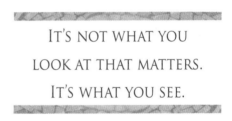

IT'S NOT WHAT YOU LOOK AT THAT MATTERS. IT'S WHAT YOU SEE.

of the people in it, an honest look might reveal that the reactions we have to things and people give us more information about ourselves than about what we see. Perhaps, if we really want to see change in the world and find a common, sacred meeting place, we can practice forgiveness rather than against-ness.

Daily Forgiveness
Process Reminders

For a more detailed explanation
of the Daily Forgiveness Process Guidelines, see pages 45–46.

1. Find a quiet place where you will not be disturbed for at least 30 to 60 minutes.

2. Still your mind for at least 5 minutes or listen to the *Stillness Meditation*.

3. Listen to the *Forgiveness Prayer* on the accompanying audio program. Then read the Forgiveness Prayer, once silently and once aloud.

4. Scan the Emotional Trigger List on pages 9–14.

5. Write out the 12 Forgiveness Statements for each day's topic on thinking, judging, and believing in your Forgiveness Journal (Days 1–18). Write your Forgiveness Letters (Days 19–21).

6. Perform your Pro EFT™ Forgiveness Tapping Sequences.

7. Process thoughts and feelings consciously through your Forgiveness Journal Reflections.

8. Listen to the *Gratitude Meditation*.

9. Complete the day's practice in quiet reflection or with meditative music.

10. Be sure to do something good for yourself today!

I Forgive Myself for Judging the World

Today's forgiveness practice addresses our grievances, disappointments, criticisms, and upsets with the world at large. This includes the government, social systems, religious organizations, specific leaders, and the changing policies that affect the public in general, and perhaps you specifically. While we may not recognize how our pet peeves and criticisms about society at large affect our lives, any upset held in consciousness needs to be forgiven.

Remember, all thoughts are energy. All energy creates. Anything that we think about will have an effect. Just as we must forgive ourselves for judging specific people and personal experiences, we can and must release the pent-up energy, upsets, and silent complaints about our world. Releasing any toxic energy that we hold in our minds or hearts opens us to more positive energy and experiences. There is no harmless judgment. If you have a judgment or limiting belief about anyone or anything, forgiveness is required. Today's practice provides an opportunity to say what you could not say, were afraid to say, or perhaps thought no one cared to hear.

A Prayer of Forgiveness

Dear God:

Today, I come to You asking that You open my mind, my heart, my eyes, and my ears to Your presence in the world I see. Today, I ask to think only the thoughts that I think with You and to see You in all people and circumstances. I confess that I have been critical of people and situations that may affect my life in ways I do not always understand. I confess that I have held judgments about people with whom I do not agree and about things that I do not accept. I confess that in certain situations, under certain circumstances, I have been critical, demeaning, and dismissive of people, their opinions, and convictions when they do not mirror what I believe. I have fought to be right about what I believe while judging other people wrong about what they believe. I confess I have engaged in the energy of against-ness, harbored upsets, and uttered criticisms that have been unkind, unloving, and in some cases attacking as a way to justify a position held in my mind. Today, I ask to be forgiven for it all as I forgive others. Today, I choose to see the world and all people with the eyes of love, acceptance, and peace.

I lay down all of my weapons today.

I rest in Thee today.

I let it be!

And so it is!

THE FORGIVEness

DAY 18
Journal Work

I Forgive
the World

– I Forgive My Mind for Thinking –

EXAMPLE

I forgive my mind for thinking that all politicians are crooks who do not serve the people who elected them.

I forgive my mind for thinking _____

about _____

I forgive my mind for thinking _____

about _____

I forgive my mind for thinking _____

about _____

I forgive my mind for thinking _____

about _____

– I FORGIVE MY MIND FOR JUDGING –

EXAMPLE

I forgive myself for judging the world for the terrorists that it never captures.

I forgive myself for judging the world for

_____

_____

I forgive myself for judging the world because

_____

_____

I forgive myself for judging the world when

_____

_____

I forgive myself for judging the world when

_____

_____

– I FORGIVE MYSELF FOR BELIEVING –

EXAMPLE

I forgive myself for believing that all people who receive government aid are lazy and undeserving.

I forgive myself for believing
_____

about
_____

I forgive myself for believing
_____

about
_____

I forgive myself for believing
_____

about
_____

I forgive myself for believing
_____

about
_____

– TAPPING SEQUENCE –

Review Basic Tapping Sequence Guidelines on pages 53–59.

1. Review each of the day's 12 Forgiveness Statements out loud. This will help you identify the specific aspects of the issue that you want to tap on.

2. Rate the intensity level of any unforgiveness you hold about today's topic on a scale of 1 to 10. Write the number down.

3. Neutralize all subconscious resistance. Repeat a Reversal Statement 3 times while tapping continuously on the Karate Chop point.

4. Focus on the issue you'll be tapping on. Repeat a Set-Up Statement 3 times while tapping continuously on the Karate Chop point.

5. Tap 7 times on each of the 10 meridian points while repeating out loud the key details from the 12 Forgiveness Statements. This process can be modeled on the bonus Tapping Scripts.

6. Recheck the intensity level of any unforgiveness you hold about today's topic. Write the number down. If the level is at 8 or higher, repeat the entire sequence. If the level is less than 8, tap on a Modified Set-Up Statement, then perform the 10-point Tapping Sequence on your 12 Forgiveness Statements until you are at a 0 level of intensity.

– REFLECTIONS –

_____

_____

_____

_____

_____

_____

_____

_____

_____

_____

_____

_____

_____

_____

Forgiveness is not an occasional act, it is a constant attitude.

—MARTIN LUTHER KING, JR.

Congratulations, Beloved!

You are now entering the final stages of your forgiveness practice. Now that you have forgiven yourself for the judgments and limiting beliefs you have held, the time has come to ask for and claim forgiveness from others. For the final three days of your practice, you will be writing Forgiveness Letters to specific people from whom you require forgiveness. You are not required to mail these letters, nor will you need to speak to the people involved about this practice. The purpose of these letters is to provide you with yet another opportunity to clear your mind and heart of any lingering toxic residue. Having forgiven yourself, asking for and claiming forgiveness from others is the next essential step in your total healing.

You are encouraged to complete one letter a day for the next three days, to anyone, including yourself, from whom you need forgiveness. Once you have completed the letter, you are encouraged to transform it by burning it, burying in, tearing it into pieces, flushing it, or deleting it from your computer. With any of these actions, you are not destroying the letter. Instead, you are transforming it and the energy it carries. As you write each letter, you are encouraged to have a clear and irreversible intention to be healed.

*T*here are many ways that I have hurt and harmed others, have betrayed or abandoned them, caused them suffering, knowingly or unknowingly, out of my pain, fear, anger, and confusion. Let yourself remember and visualize the ways you have hurt others. See the pain you have caused out of your own fear and confusion. Feel your own sorrow and regret. Sense that finally you can release this burden and ask for forgiveness. Take as much time as you need to picture each memory that still burdens your heart. And then as each person comes to mind, gently say: "I ask for your forgiveness, I ask for your forgiveness."

—JACK KORNFIELD,
THE ART OF FORGIVENESS,
LOVINGKINDNESS, AND PEACE

TODAY, I ASK FOR AND CLAIM FORGIVENESS FOR MYSELF

Forgiveness
Letter 1

Dear _____ :

I now ask for and claim your forgiveness for every unkind, unloving thought I have held about or against you.

I forgive myself for judging you for _____

_____

I forgive myself for judging you when _____

_____

I forgive myself for judging you because _____

_____

I forgive myself for judging you as _____

_____

I now ask for and claim your forgiveness for judging you about _____

_____

I now ask for and claim your forgiveness for judging you when

_____

_____

I now ask for and claim your forgiveness for judging you because

_____

_____

I now ask for and claim your forgiveness for judging you as

_____

_____

I forgive any and all judgments you have held about me or against me. All is clear between us now. We are both free to live our lives as divine expressions of our Creator. I bless you, and I release you. I bless myself, and I claim my freedom.

And So It Is!

Signature _____   Date _____

Not to forgive is to be imprisoned by the past, by old grievances that do not permit life to proceed with new business. Not to
forgive is to yield oneself to another's control . . . to be locked into
a sequence of act and response, of outrage and revenge, tit for
tat, escalating always. The present is endlessly overwhelmed and
devoured by the past. Forgiveness frees the forgiver. It extracts the
forgiver from someone else's nightmare.

—LANCE MORROW,
THE CHIEF:
A MEMOIR OF FATHERS AND SONS

Today, I Ask for and Claim Forgiveness for Myself

Forgiveness Letter 2

Dear _____ :

I now ask for and claim your forgiveness for every unkind, unloving thought I have held about or against you.

I forgive myself for judging you for _____

_____

I forgive myself for judging you when _____

_____

I forgive myself for judging you because _____

_____

I forgive myself for judging you as _____

_____

I now ask for and claim your forgiveness for judging you about _____

_____

I now ask for and claim your forgiveness for judging you when

_____

_____

I now ask for and claim your forgiveness for judging you because

_____

_____

I now ask for and claim your forgiveness for judging you as

_____

_____

I forgive any and all judgments you have held about me or against me. All is clear between us now. We are both free to live our lives as divine expressions of our Creator. I bless you, and I release you. I bless myself, and I claim my freedom.

And So It Is!

Signature _____   Date _____

*B*efore you can live a part of you has to die. You have to let go of what could have been, how you should have acted and what you wish you would have said differently. You have to accept that you can't change the past experiences, opinions of others at that moment in time or outcomes from their choices or yours. When you finally recognize that truth then you will understand the true meaning of forgiveness of yourself and others.

—SHANNON L. ALDER

Today, I Ask for and Claim Forgiveness for Myself

Forgiveness Letter 3

Dear _____ :

I now ask for and claim your forgiveness for every unkind, unloving thought I have held about or against you.

I forgive myself for judging you for _____

_____

I forgive myself for judging you when _____

_____

I forgive myself for judging you because _____

_____

I forgive myself for judging you as _____

_____

I now ask for and claim your forgiveness for judging you about ___

_____

I now ask for and claim your forgiveness for judging you when

_____

_____

I now ask for and claim your forgiveness for judging you because

_____

_____

I now ask for and claim your forgiveness for judging you as

_____

_____

I forgive any and all judgments you have held about me or against me. All is clear between us now. We are both free to live our lives as divine expressions of our Creator. I bless you, and I release you. I bless myself, and I claim my freedom.

And So It Is!

Signature _____   Date _____

Acknowledgments

With love and gratitude, I would like to thank and acknowledge my beloved and supportive editor, Cheryl Woodruff; my manager, Rodney Scott; and my dear friend and longtime attorney, Kenneth L. Browning. Nothing I do in the world would be possible without the support and encouragement of the faculty of the Inner Visions Institute. I would like to express my deepest love and appreciation to Almasi Wilcots, Rev. Helen Jones, Rev. Elease Welch, Rev. Nancy Yeates, Rev. Terrie Bowling, Rev. Deanna Mathias, Rev. Lydia Ayo Mu'Ashe Ruiz, Rev. Deborah Chinaza Lee, Ken and Renée Kizer, Robert Pruitt, Jackie Smith, Rev. Rosetta Hillary, Jackie Smith, Rev. Maxine Legall, Charlotte Wilson, Rev. Tammy Manly, Rev. Irene Oyabumi Robinson, Rev. Candas Ifama Barnes, Rev. Carmen Gonzalez, Rev. Cathy Chioma Gaynor and the IVISD God Squad, Danni Stillwell, Yahfaw Shacor, Min. Laura Rawlings, Rev. Lizelle Robinson, Janet Barner, and Ebun Adelona. Barbara Perkins, thank you for steering the ship into the next port.

To my friend and brother, Ben Dowling, a master musician, I thank you for the generosity of your spirit and for allowing me to share your music with the world. The notes, chords, and harmony of your soul lend to a miraculous completion of the project.

To my brother, friend, and teacher Frank Ellis, whom I have never met face-to-face, thank you for guiding me through the beauty of *A Course in Miracles*. The four years we have spent together on the pages of my e-mails have been some of the sweetest times of my life. You are a true gem in God's crown.

To my friend and Coach Lindsay Kenny, for giving a new lease on life and a process that makes me a permanent tenant in all of the goodness life has to offer. Words cannot adequately convey the depths of my gratitude. I say thank you, but I am also tapping about how much I love and appreciate you.

I would also like to thank the entire production team of *Iyanla: Fix My Life* for holding the vision and supporting the work I do in the world. Thank you, Sherri Salata, Eric Logan, Jill VanLokeren, Jon Sinclair, Robert Wesley Branch, Terry Goulder, Cela Sutton, Erica Bryant, Kelly Jansen, Naha Datt, Arelene Wilkinson, Gillian Carter, Maya Alexander, Danny Beers, Lori Read, Rachel Winn, Julie Anderson, Julie Maisel, Dana Brooks, and of course Ms. Oprah Winfrey.

To my children Damon and Nisa, you are the wind beneath my wings. Thank you for choosing me to usher you into life. To my grandchildren Asholae, Oluwa, Niamoja, Adesola, Kimani, Xavier, David, Onaje, and the baby girl Iyanni, I just want you to know I love you.

Ms. Chavon Kells, you are simply the best. My BFF Rev. Shaheerah Stevens; my spiritual mother Raina Bundy, and my Godfather Awo Oshun Kunle, your prayers are my oxygen. To the members of my Ile' LaTonia Taylor, Herman, Suzette and Kimberly Perry, Aldo V. Clarke, Ronald King Sheppard, and Adegbola Nobles, thank for always being willing to take second place. Finally, to you Oluku'se C.M. Plaskett, for every trip to every airport, regardless of the time, I thank you!

Bonus Content

Thank you for purchasing *Forgiveness* by Iyanla Vanzant. This product includes a free download! To access this bonus content, please visit www.hayhouse.com/download and enter the Product ID and Download Code as they appear below.

Product ID: 8367
Download Code: ebook

For further assistance, please contact Hay House Customer Care by phone: US (800) 654-5126 or INTL CC+(760) 431-7695 or visit www.hayhouse.com/contact.php.

Thank you again for your Hay House purchase. Enjoy!
Hay House, Inc. • P.O. Box 5100 • Carlsbad, CA 92018 • (800) 654-5126

FORGIVENESS AUDIO DOWNLOAD TRACK LIST

1. Introduction
2. Daily Forgiveness Process Guidelines
3. Stillness Meditation
4. Gratitude Meditation
5. Bonus: Forgiveness Meditation
6. Day 1: I Forgive Myself
7. Day 2: I Forgive My Body
8. Day 3: I Forgive My Life
9. Day 4: I Forgive My Mother
10. Day 5: I Forgive My Father
11. Day 6: I Forgive God
12. Day 7: I Forgive My Feelings
13. Day 8: I Forgive My Weaknesses and Failures
14. Day 9: I Forgive My Choices
15. Day 10: I Forgive My Relationship with Money

MUSIC CREDITS

Piano music by Ben Dowling from his album, *The Path of Peace*. A gifted pianist, improviser, composer, and synthesist for Grammy- and Academy Award–winning artists, Ben is a "musician's musician." This extraordinary artist embraces musical improvisation as a spiritual practice. For more on the man and his beautiful music, visit: bendowling.com.

Introduction: "Reflecting Pool" by Royalty Free Music

Daily Forgiveness Practice: "In Passing" (5:57) ©2009 Ben Dowling (bendowling.com) and Visionsound Music ASCAP

Stillness Meditation: (breath setup) "Twilight Comes" by Royalty Free Music, into (meditation) "Exploration" (3:40) ©2009 Ben Dowling (bendowling.com) and Visionsound Music ASCAP

Gratitude Meditation: "Peace Be Still" by Royalty Free Music

Forgiveness Meditation: (breath setup) "Intimacy" by Royalty Free Music, into (meditation) "In Passing" (5:57) ©2009 Ben Dowling (bendowling.com) and Visionsound Music ASCAP

Days 1 through 18: "Somber Memories" by Royalty Free Music

Caution: This audio program features meditation/visualization exercises that render it inappropriate for use while driving or operating heavy machinery.

Publisher's note: Hay House and SmileyBooks products are intended to be powerful, inspirational, and life-changing tools for personal growth and healing. They are not intended as a substitute for medical care. Please use this audio program under the supervision of your care provider. Neither the author, SmileyBooks, nor Hay House, Inc., assumes any responsibility for your improper use of this product.

Copyright Extension

© Andreas Branch

ABOUT THE AUTHOR

Iyanla Vanzant is one of the country's most prolific writers and public speakers and among the most influential, socially engaged, and acclaimed spiritual life coaches of our time. Host and executive producer of the break-out hit *Iyanla: Fix My Life* on OWN: Oprah Winfrey Network, Iyanla Vanzant's focus on faith, empowerment, and loving relationships has inspired millions around the world. A woman of passion, vision, and purpose, Iyanla is also the co-founder and executive director of Inner Visions Institute for Spiritual Development.

Website: www.Iyanla.com

SMILEYBOOKS TITLES
OF RELATED INTEREST

TRUST: Mastering the Four Essential Trusts
by Iyanla Vanzant

IF YOU CAN SEE IT, YOU CAN BE IT: 12 Street Smart Recipes for Success
by Chef Jeff Henderson

ALMOST WHITE: Forced Confessions of a Latino in Hollywood
by Rick Najera

THE RICH AND THE REST OF US: A Poverty Manifesto
by Tavis Smiley and Cornel West

HEALTH FIRST: The Black Women's Wellness Guide
by Eleanor Hinton Hoytt and Hilary Beard

PEACE FROM BROKEN PIECES: How to Get Through What You're Going Through
by Iyanla Vanzant

TOO IMPORTANT TO FAIL: Saving America's Boys
by Tavis Smiley Reports

BRAINWASHED: Challenging the Myth of Black Inferiority
by Tom Burrell

All of the above are available at your local bookstore,
or may be ordered online through Hay House (see next page).

LIFECLASS
PRESENTS
FORGIVENESS
WITH IYANLA
HOW TO FORGIVE EVERYONE FOR EVERYTHING
AVAILABLE AT
OWNLIFECLASSES.COM/FORGIVENESS